Foreword

Blogging can be a solitary, soul-sapping ex[...] it, apart from the obvious fact that I like writi[...] almost daily basis, I am still here, and I have [...] answer is probably that the positive feedback [...] [...] the negative feedback has been quite sparse thankfully, th[...] [...] odd "call yourself a journalist?!" line makes me chuckle (for the record: no, I don't. Obviously).

My football club have also been amazingly generous to us City bloggers. I have had free tickets to their CityLive pre-season party, a free City Legends tour round the ground and training facilities and best of all, was invited onto the second parade bus that crawled down Deansgate with the players and trophies just a few months ago. That was an experience that money cannot buy. The club's inclusive policy and their willingness to embrace social media and look after their own has helped me keep going.

Deep down there's that desire to make some sort of living out of one of the few things I enjoy doing, but that is almost certainly a pipe dream. So I got to thinking if there was another way of getting something more from writing. It was then that an idea popped into my head, and has remained there ever since. That idea was to release some past thoughts in book-form for a good cause, rather than to release some thoughts to pay for my real ale consumption. I thought about it for a while, wondering what my true motives were. Was I being selfless or actually selfish by sub-consciously trying to raise my profile? Then I saw a cause that made me shout at myself to stop thinking too much about everything and just bloody do it. If I can make some money for a good cause, who gives a damn what the motives are? It will make me feel better, it will give me satisfaction and I would feel like I was doing something really constructive. They are good enough reasons, especially the last one.

So here is a selection of stuff I have written since I discovered Twitter, since Manchester City won the lottery and since Manchester United fans had to adjust to a brave new world. I wanted it to be an enjoyable read so I have included just the humorous articles I published in the previous three years, and I include in this category some of the worst articles I have read from our wonderful tabloid press over the past few years, as whilst they weren't intended as humorous pieces, their pathetic reasoning certainly made me and many others laugh. it soon became clear that whilst I try to avoid taking pot shots at City's illustrious neighbours, most of my shots came in these lighter pieces. Thus this book appears rather anti-United, a book written through blue blinkers, but it is not serious, and it's for a good cause, so if any United fan does read this, bite your lip and have a laugh at yourself, otherwise I shall bring down a curse on you for all eternity. The truth is, any criticism of United is usually not directed at the club itself but the media coverage of said club, which can veer from parody to adulation to fawning but, like any other club, can also lead to unfair criticism and hatchet jobs/prejudices.

On a separate note, apologies for the odd repetition, proof-reading is not my forté......

Enjoy my ramblings, retweet on Twitter, share on Facebook and do some good....but first a few important words on what buying this book contributes towards....

The Charities

Choosing a charity to support is difficult – there are ten thousand at a bare minimum that I'd be happy to donate to. Every charity needs as much money as possible, especially in these austere times. For this book I wanted to support something different, away from the norm. The first choice was easy, one of many charities that deals with an illness most don't know exist so perhaps doesn't get the attention it merits. It has affected the daughter of a colleague over the past couple of years and the support received from the foundation mentioned later was invaluable.

Neurofibromatosis is the name for a number of genetic conditions that cause tumours to grow along your nerves. There are two main types of neurofibromatosis:

•Neurofibromatosis type 1 (NF1) is the most common type of neurofibromatosis, affecting about one in 3,000 births.
•Neurofibromatosis type 2 (NF2) is a less common type of neurofibromatosis, affecting about one in 35,000 births.
Despite sharing the same name, these two types of neurofibromatosis are separate conditions with different symptoms and caused by changes in different genes.
NF1 is a condition you are born with, although some symptoms develop gradually over many years. The severity of the condition can vary considerably from person to person.

In most cases of NF1 the skin is affected. About one in three people with NF1 also develop a range of further health problems, including:
•high blood pressure
•a curved spine (scoliosis)
•learning difficulties and behavioural problems
•a type of cancer known as malignant peripheral nerve sheath tumours, which affects around 10% of people with NF1 over their lifetime

There is currently no cure for NF1. Instead, people with the condition are regularly monitored for further problems and treated if and when these develop.
This can involve surgery to remove tumours and improve bone abnormalities, medication to control secondary conditions such as high blood pressure, and therapy for behavioural problems.
In many cases, careful monitoring and treatment can help people with NF1 live a full life. However, there is a risk of developing serious problems such as strokes and some types of cancer, which can reduce life expectancy in some people by up to 15 years.

Almost everyone with NF2 will develop tumours on the nerves responsible for hearing and balance. These typically cause symptoms such as:

•gradual hearing loss, that usually gets worse over time
•ringing or buzzing in the ears (tinnitus)
•balance problems, particularly when moving in the dark or walking on uneven ground

Tumours can also develop inside the brain or spinal cord, or the nerves to the arms and legs. This can cause symptoms such as weakness in the arms and legs and persistent headaches.

NF2 is caused by a genetic mutation. This is where the instructions that are carried in all living cells become scrambled in some way. As a result, the growth of nerve tissue is not controlled properly. Again, there is currently no cure for NF2. Treatment involves regular monitoring and treating any problems that occur.

Surgery can be used to remove most tumours, although there is a risk this will cause problems such as complete deafness or facial weakness.
Most people with NF2 eventually develop significant hearing loss and often benefit from learning to lip read or using a hearing aid. Sometimes, special implants can be inserted to aid hearing.

NF2 tends to get worse over time, although the speed at which this happens can vary considerably. However, most people with NF2 will eventually lose their hearing and some people will require a wheelchair or other type of mobility device.

Tumours that develop inside the brain and spinal cord can place a strain on the body and shorten life expectancy. The average life expectancy for someone with NF2 is 65 years of age.

Here's some blurb from the Neuro Foundation's website:
Everyday a baby is born in the UK with Neurofibromatosis. There are over 25,000 people in the UK affected by the condition and as yet, there is no cure.

The Neuro Foundation's work includes funding a team of Specialist Advisors and a Telephone Helpline, as well as supporting research and raising awareness about Neurofibromatosis.

Our Advisors have a depth of knowledge and understanding of neurofibromatosis which benefits individuals, families and professionals needing their expertise.

Our Vision

To improve the lives of those affected by neurofibromatosis.
We work in collaboration with the NCG funded service to achieve this.

Our Mission

To enable people concerned about neurofibromatosis to find solutions appropriate to them.
The charity delivers its mission through five services to members, supporters and beneficiaries. It endeavours to :
•Inform – We provide accurate, relevant and up to date information that explains the conditions of NF1 and NF2, the implications, challenges and opportunities, in language understood by all.

•Advise – We provide practical and emotional advice to help people find the best services and support available. We enable people to make choices about how they approach and live with neurofibromatosis.
•Advocate – We aim to increase knowledge, awareness and understanding of NF, and will campaign for change in areas we believe will improve the lives of those affected by neurofibromatosis.
•Connect – We aim to take a pivotal role in bringing together groups of people interested in neurofibromatosis to maximise the support and information available to them.
•Fund – We seek to make funds available for small projects to bodies and patient groups where we believe it will make a difference.

http://www.nfauk.org/

As for the second choice, and as to whether I should even have more than one choice, a lovely advert watched whilst I mulled this all over made up my mind for me, so my second charity is Macmillan Cancer Support. I hope I never have to see a single member of their staff (no offence) , but I have heard enough stories about the wonderful level of care and support they provide and I do not recall donating to them before, so it too became an easy choice.

Here's their blurb:
When you have cancer, you don't just worry about what will happen to your body, you worry about what will happen to your life.

At Macmillan, we know how a cancer diagnosis can affect everything and we're here to support you through. From help with money worries and advice about work, to someone who'll listen if you just want to talk, we'll be there.

We'll help you make the choices you need to take back control, so you can start to feel like yourself again.

No one should face cancer alone. We want to reach and improve the lives of every one of those people

http://www.macmillan.org.uk/Aboutus/AboutUsHome.aspx

Enjoy the book, and thank you.

**A Little Book of (hopefully funny) Manchester City Stories
2008-14: The Golden Years**

Manchester City – nobody knows their name, or so the song went. Well since 2008, everybody has known their name. With an increased profile comes increased scrutiny, and like fans of most teams, I developed a certain level of paranoia at the media treatment of my club once it came into money. Most fans think the newspapers have it in for their team, so it was a natural progression for me really. Before Carlos Tevez and Mario Balotelli were making headlines for all the wrong reasons, Emmanuel Adebayor, a £25m signing from Arsenal, was doing his bit to hog the headlines, namely when playing against his old side, running the length of the pitch to celebrate a goal in front of foaming Arsenal fans, and taking a swipe at Robin Van Persie. Annoyed at the hysterical coverage of such incidents, I wrote a short story containing the real responses in the media to the incidents.

Burn Him
(names have been changed to protect the guilty – the quotes have not)

The father tucked his young son into bed.
"What story would you like tonight, son. Perhaps a comic? Or how about a legend from not very long, long ago?"
The boys eyes widened.
"A legend please dad!"
"Ok, son. And when I say legend, I should point out that this story is entirely true. Only the names have been changed, to protect the innocent."
"Ok!"
The young child took a sip of his Carlos Queiroz cocoa™.
"Not very long, long ago, there was a man called Manuel Adebuy-your. Manuel was from a small country a long way away called Tango. He used to play football for a team called Arsenal Wanderers, but they booed their players a lot, so he moved to a new club called Madchester Rovers, who had lots of money, and liked to brag about it."
"Did everyone hate them dad?"
"Yes they did son. They had no class, and no history, unlike their neighbours across the road, who had all those things, and a quiet dignity and humility that all the gold in Abu Derby Doo could not buy."
"They sound horrible!"
"Oh they were. Anyway, Manuel got to play against his old club. Another player, called Van Persil, tried to hurt him so nasty Manuel kicked him in the head as he slid by. This made the other team mad. Then Manuel scored a goal and celebrated in front of the mad team's fans. This made the mad team's fans mad. They threw stuff at Manuel, including certain items of fruit, but we won't mention that again."
"Madchester Rovers won the game, but the other team were very bad losers, so they started crying and their biggest cry baby of all, Van Persil, made a statement on the club's website saying how hurt he was by the challenge. This player had previously

been sent off for kicking an opponent in the head and walking up to a goalkeeper and elbowing him to the floor."

"What's a website dad?"

"It's what people used to use to communicate with each other before humans developed mind-reading abilities."

"It sounds rubbish dad."

"It had its uses. Anyway, soon Sky Sports News got hold of the story."

"Wow dad, were they around a long time ago?!"

"Yes son, though they weren't owned by Manchester United in those days. Not officially, anyway."

The father chuckled.

"Now Sky were under the thumb of the 'Big Four' Football clubs – Arsenal Wanderers, Madchester Etihad, Kidneypool and Chelski. The last thing they wanted to do was upset the most powerful clubs, so they had decided that the kick by Manuel was the worst in the history of football, which began in 1992."

"Worse than Alan Shearer's kick on Lennon?"

"That was an accident son."

"What about all Rooney's kicks at players dad?"

"If you took out his passion for the game, he would have been half the player. So those kicks had to be put into context son."

"What about when Chris Morgan fractured the skull of the Barnsley player, almost killing him?"

The father was impressed by his 6-year-old son's detailed knowledge of legendary footballing incidents.

"The referee booked him son. You can't go charging players afterwards and undermine the referee. Well, unless you play in Sky blue of course!"

The father laughed. The son frowned.

"Anyway, Sky decided to run with the story for the rest of the week. They called it a stamp, even though it clearly wasn't. They showed the foul every ten minutes, from multiple angles. They wheeled into the studio endless ex-referees, managers and ex-players to condemn Manuel. They even interviewed the FA Chairman who condemned the tackle. He just happened, by pure coincidence to support Arsenal Wanderers."

"That doesn't seem very fair, dad."

"Life isn't son, life isn't. Well, unless you're in the Champions League every year, then life is very fair indeed."

"Anyway, by Monday the witch-hunt was still continuing and now the possible ban was up to 10 matches. Maybe even prison. I mean, if he'd done that in the street..."

"Don't be silly dad!"

"Some people actually think like that son. During all of this, there had still been no mention of Van Persil's goal celebration, his lunge on Adebuy-your that resulted in the alleged stamp, or the Arsenal Wanderers players spending the match trying to hack Manuel down, including three attempts during one mazy run."

"Why was that dad?"

"It's to do with agendas son. When you're older, I'll explain in more detail."

"Ok."

"You see son, the Wanderers fans booed their own players quite a lot, so there was no reason not to after they had left, and they hated Manuel because he had courted another team called Intra Melan. Fabbygas himself had courted a team called Barcyloner every summer, but that was ok with the fans of the Wanderers."

"Now, it wasn't long before the Premier League chief executive, a Mr Dick Scoobymore, had his say as well. You see son, Madchester Rovers had already been accused of killing football. And now individual players were killing it too, according to Dick. He said: 'We've had a fantastic two days of football, and that includes the game at Eastlands. Why then, when you run the Premier League, would you want the headlines on Sunday through to Monday being something else? You don't want it, do you? So clearly it doesn't do any good for the brand that is football in one sense. You'd rather it didn't happen. Of course when these instances come up you'd rather that the talk was about the action and the goals.'"

"Dick couldn't see the irony of how him talking about it even more was simply exacerbating the situation."
His son nodded his head. He had no idea what exacerbated meant though.
"Soon, the police were involved, what with Manuel's terrible, riot-inducing goal celebration and all that. Former Met Police commander John O'Connor said: 'I am sure the police will want Adebuy-your to be made an example of. From a police perspective, Adebuy-your could have been arrested and then charged with actual body harm for the incident with Van Persil. He would then have faced the prospect of standing trial in court.'"
"But dad he never touched anyone!"
"Don't worry son, remember, this is just a story!"
"Oh, yes. Ok!"
"No one would actually say that!"
"But dad, wasn't he booked by the referee at the time. Shouldn't that have been the end of it?"
"Of course son. The rules were quite clear on this. Under the FIFA Laws of the Game, the FA is prohibited from taking disciplinary action when incidents are seen at the time by the match officials.
An FA spokesman once said: 'The Football Association can only take action in the case of incidents that are not seen by officials.
"Whilst it is clear that the officials did not see the full extent of the incident, they did see players coming together and to take any further action would be tantamount to re-refereeing the game and this would be contrary to the laws of the game.' And thus son when a Mr Bosingwa kicked a Mr Benayoun in back - no charge. When a Mr Rooney kicks opponents? No charge. When that nasty Mr Barton karate kicked Etuhu - no charge. You see, they had a nice little get out clause whereby the referee could say he dealt with it at the time, or he could say he didn't even though he obviously did, so that the player could be charged."
"So dad, the police would ignore the behaviour of the Arsenal fans, and all sporting precedents in rugby and football, and waste the public's money in bringing a prosecution against a footballer for running along a pitch and then sliding on his knees but would then walk free as any case would involve reasonable doubt being easily established, something that the FA do not bother themselves with in their 'Kangaroo Court'?"
The father patted his son's head.
"Well done – you're a quick learner! And such a wide vocabulary for a 6-year-old!"
"Everyone wanted their say though, son. There was a journalist called Simone Hattenstone, who ridiculously claimed to be a Madchester fan. He said "If even now

all he wants to do is take out his revenge with his studs and provoke crowds into riots what's he going to be like when things go bad?"

Ex-player Raymond Parlour said "Adebuy-your really owes Arsenal something for bringing him up", even though he had appeared in champions league final squad before then, as if Arsenal were some sort of charity who signed players out of the goodness of their hearts."

"That's probably why they never won anything dad!" The child laughed.

"Oliver Holts compared it to Cantona's kung-fu moment. Alan Greene said the book should be thrown at Adebuy-your - having admitted he hadn't seen the incident. Allies though came from the strangest of places. That horrible nasty man Raymond Keane stuck up for Manuel and even Patrick Barclay said 'Fans lose their right to be offended when they go on the offensive. If they cannot take it — these miserable products of a sick society who consider a player's family fair game for the vilest insults and yet, because of their numbers, are allowed to continue to serve as football's audience — they should not give it."

"Stan Collybore said Manuel should have got a 2 match ban for the goal celebration alone. Bobby Gouldd said that the whole affair would lose England their World Cup bid. These were worrying times."

"But anyway, he got a three match ban – City reluctantly accepted it. And that is the end."

The father turned the page over, and was about to close the book....

"Oh, hang on, it wasn't…"

"Come Thursday and the press had moved onto his foul on Fabbygas. Sky showed super-slo-mos of it from 15 different angles for 2 days. Soon other incidents were mentioned. Now he had slapped Songe, and it was feared that it wouldn't be long before an altercation in the tunnel involving a ball boy and the theft of his pocket money suddenly came to light to add a couple more games to his ban. And still there was no condemnation of the Van Persil lunge, or the three players that tried to cut Adeby-your in two during his mazy run."

"The opinions kept coming. Manchester United legend Alexandre Stepney believed Emmanuel Adebuy-your got off lightly with a three match ban. 'I seem to remember George Best got a six-week ban in 1970 for knocking the ball out of a referee's hands so I think Adebayor did get off lightly. These incidents are more noticeable nowadays.' You couldn't argue with logic like that, son."

"So was that finally the end, dad?"

"Well, almost son. Manuel still had to be punished for the goal celebration. You see an Arsenal player had done the same thing in front of their biggest rivals Tottingham Warmspurs just a few years previously. There had been no outcry, or punishment, because the Warmspurs fans had decided not to riot. In the end, Manuel got a nice little fine, and a suspended ban."

"And that's the end, dad?"

"Very nearly. Well, not quite. Henry Vinter, another pompous journalist out of touch with the real world, felt the punishment was nowhere near severe enough. He said: 'So whose emotion do you want most in football? A multi-millionaire itinerant footballer crowing in the face of erstwhile employers who nurtured him, paid him handsomely and cherished him until he was tempted away by riches elsewhere, or fans momentarily allowing their passions to run away with them in defending their club? Thursday's decision by the Football Association not to punish Manuel Adebuy-your for inciting Arsenal supporters at Middle Eastlands on Sept 12 is devoid of logic, defies police evidence and makes a mockery of its chief executive's stance. The case of Adebuy-your versus Arsenal forms part of a broader debate about player-fan dynamics. The Madchester Rovers forward's defence was that he had been pilloried by Arsenal fans and had a right to be emotional when scoring against them. In return, Arsenal supporters argued that Adebuy-your, painfully unprofessional in key moments, such as the Champions League semi-final last season, had shown a lack of respect to the club that helped make him. Adebuy-your's subsequent contemptuous comments about Arsenal, particularly the fans, inevitably heated the emotions of those entering the away section of Middle Eastlands. Just as every village has an idiot, every support harbours some unpleasant types, yet anyone with any experience of travelling around the nation's many grounds will agree that Arsenal's following is one of the less threatening.Some yobs rushed to the front, faces disfigured with hate, as Adebuy-your celebrated his goal in front of them and Arsenal can certainly do without them. But Adebuy-your is paid to be there, and with that comes responsibility.

Footballers being human, allowances must be made for the intoxication of the goal scoring moment (which is why the petty rule of a caution for removing a shirt should be scrapped). From Marco Tardelli's screaming to Ryan Giggs's hairy chest and Lee Sharpe's Elvis impression, great celebrations should be, well, celebrated. But Adebuy-your crossed the line. He even crossed the halfway line in his 70-yard run to goad the Arsenal fans. In every sense, Adebuy-your went too far. A one-game ban would have reminded him and his immature peers of that. It's not difficult. Carlitos Tévez showed with his respectful approach to West Ham United fans last week, a contrast to Adebuy-your.The gut instinct of the FA's chief executive, Ian Watmore, that the governors' "Respect" campaign demanded players show some self-control was correct. Sadly, Watmore has been undermined by his own organisation. Gay Neville, so often the scourge of FA officials, was unintentionally to blame. Red Nev's Sept 20 taunting of Madchester fans was a far less splenetic offence, hardly requiring of more than a warning, yet his escape set a precedent, allowing Adebuy-your to follow him over the wire. The FA has stupidly stoked the home fires for Adebuy-your's visit to the Emirates on April 24. Now that will be emotional.
"But dad, anyone with a brain knows West Ham fans like Tevez!"
"Yes son, anyone with a brain. Unfortunately in times of legend, the people paid to write tended not to engage their brains first. And then we come back to agendas. But that is for another time."
The father tucked his son up in bed, and turned off the light. As he left the room, his son said:
"Dad, what happened to Madchester Rovers in the end?"
"Well son, they became very successful. The people in the press had to change their attitude, because of their success. And their fans finally saw some trophies come to Middle Eastlands."
"And did the club find some humility and dignity?"
"No son, money can't buy you that."

With the investment, as I may have mentioned already, came intense criticism. This was to be expected, but what soon stood out was the particular narratives that people used when attacking the club and the money they were now spending. Here's a handy list I wrote that can be printed off and laminated should you get trapped in a pub with a rival fan.

The Bumper Bundle of City Slurs

The sheikhs will get bored. This was the default setting for the anti-City brigade in the early months and years of the new regime, but you may still see the odd straggler pop up every now and then with the same claim, their desperation tangible. The construction of one of the world's premier academies has rather scuppered this argument, as has the announcement this week of the club-backed plan to build 7000 homes on wasteland near the ground.

How can City spend so much money during a recession? My personal favourite this one. Never mind that every second, City players' wages are making the government money, every ticket sold makes the government VAT, never mind that owners from Abu Dhabi aren't responsible for the British economy, never mind that they are regenerating a swathe of east Manchester, the bulls**t mountain peaked soon after the takeover when Mark Lawrenson commented that City's money could be used to build hospitals, whilst Mike Calvin opined that the Sheikh should take over FCUM (see articles elsewhere for the full, gory details).

Spent a billion pounds on the team. Textbook figure-spinning here, as repeated by prize buffoon Brian Reade this week. You will have read 100 times about City's billion pound team. It is nothing of the sort of course, as a billion pounds is the total investment in the club by the owners, including huge building projects and naturally the figure ignores income from sales and suchlike. But it's such a nice, big, round figure for the world's dimwits to quote.

City are the Sheikh's "plaything". As a kid I had a lego fire station and Subbuteo. Sheikh Mansour clearly moves on different levels. To be fair, I do recall that the rich kids at my school all owned football clubs.

The oil will run out. When it does City will be royally screwed, goes the argument. When City's owner makes a couple of billion pounds in one afternoon from selling his shares in Barclays, the argument falls down somewhat.

City have bought success. Remember football before City came along and killed it? I particularly remember United's band of plucky part-timers, loanees and free transfers that swept all before them in the 1990s. Simpler times. We will all be reminded of City's buying power should Liverpool win this season's Premier League, whilst their spending, good and bad, will be consigned to history's dustbin.

You can't buy success. Some argue the opposite of the above point. Yes, yes you can, as demonstrated by United and Chelsea over the past 20 years. Repeatedly breaking the transfer record suggests otherwise doesn't it United? Paying a player £300,000 a week might not be quite successful however. Now that United have had a bad season, what will they do? Spend of course, and spend BIG.

Emptyhad. TOP BANTER KLAXON. Yep, City never sell out, apart from all those games that they have sold out, and woe betide if anyone goes to the toilet during a match as the watching nation will seize upon your naked seat in an instant. This is an argument that has transcended social media and is parroted by MEN, Guardian journalists and beyond. As news filters through that City's ground expansion will start imminently, prepare to be bored senseless by witty comments on not selling out.

City fans are bitters and liars. As shown by the previous point, the rest of this article and the season as a whole for the team across the city, I think we can now all say with some conviction who the bitters and liars are.

Most City fans used to support Chelsea. Back to the playground we go, for a claim so puerile and stupid it's hard to dissect. The sad thing is that the people who come out with this think they are actually being funny. Think about that for a moment. #Megalolz.

You can't buy class. Well indeed. Can't really argue with this. You can't buy class such as Vincent Kompany, Fernandinho, David Silva and Sergio Aguero, players who ooze class and humility on and off the pitch, but you can buy a striker banned for racist remarks, a defender banned for racist remarks, a compulsory cup scheme, owners leeching hundreds of millions out of the club, owners who change the colour of the home kit or the name of the team and you can buy £1000+ season tickets or Marione Fellaini. So yeah, spot on. If only City fans could demonstrate such vast reservoirs of class to fly a plane over the ground during a match calling for our manager to be sacked because we couldn't cope with six months without success.

All City fans have moustaches. A ridiculous claim. I know at least two City fans who don't have moustaches (hello Karen and Clara).

All City fans live in Stockport. Yet somehow we are all glory-hunters, supported Chelsea until 5 years ago and the ground is full of day-trippers, because as we all know…

Where were we when we were s**t? Nothing to say on this. Embarrassing.

City players are all mercenaries. Unlike Wayne Rooney.

City fans will ruin the minute's silence for the 50th anniversary of the Munich tragedy. One journalist demanded one policeman on the touchline for each City fan in the ground. Every other journalist demanded severe sanctions before the inevitable had even happened.
As the minutes' silence was played out impeccably, Sky turned the volume up to 11, so that you could hear a tramp shouting at a pigeon in the city centre. All to no avail.

The City fans refused to play ball and give the media the story they desperately wanted and then the team made things worse by winning.

<u>With the money they've spent....</u>
A favourite refrain of Barry Glendenning on the Guardian podcast, after which another guest usually posts a more balanced view after which Glendenning gets tongue-tied by his own flawed arguments.
Anyway, with the money City have spent, they should:
1) Have the league sewn up by Christmas
 (subsection point: "If Ferguson or Mourinho were in charge of this team", etc)
2) Win every trophy
3) Be a match for Barcelona et al
4) Be nurturing the future England team
5) Be able to sell out the occasional match
6) Not be playing Martin Demichelis, ever.

Ok, I'll give them that last one*.

*not really.

The Bumper Bundle of City Slurs: The Journalist Files (Part 1)

A long time ago, in a place not very far away, some wise men came from the east to transform an ailing football club. City fans couldn't believe their luck, and thanked every fictional god for their change of fortune. Not everyone took it so well though. Rival fans were predictably none too pleased as the death-knell was rung on football as we knew it, but plenty in the media took an instant dislike to the blues too. Here's the first part of a selection of buffoonery from Her Majesty's press over the past 6 years. Sit back and enjoy.

All excerpts in bold are my favourite bits.....

It starts with a match report. I wouldn't wipe my backside with the Sun newspaper (it would be impractical anyway), but this was the sort of coverage you could expect in the early days of the new regime. Neil Custis took a particular dislike to all Brazilians (the players at least)...

Neil Custis Match Report

*Robinho was left on the bench and as for **that waster Elano**, the sooner Hughes gets him out the better. A sub once again, Elano **pranced around like a pop diva** as he warmed up. He even kissed a young fan on the head, causing more little ones to queue up in the hope of the same. **Who on earth does he think he is?** When he and fellow Brazilian Robinho saw Ireland put City ahead on 28 minutes, they just stood still and clapped. Would you really want this pair in the trenches fighting alongside you? When Robinho finally came on just past the hour mark, he responded with one weak effort on goal. **Pathetic.***
*It is a shame he and Elano have **not got the passion that Ireland displays**.*

Others though have spent six years praying for City to fail. Bless 'em.

Ian Winwood, Daily Mirror

Dear Santa Claus,
Santa, my request this year is quite simple: I was wondering if it might be possible for you to ensure that Manchester City are relegated from the Premier League?
*....Basically, I would like Manchester City to be relegated **for the good of football itself**. I have nothing against the second team in England's third city, apart from the fact that they are the latest club to believe that the recipe for football greatness contains just one ingredient: **money**.*
*Down at the City of Manchester Stadium – the Middle Eastlands, if you prefer – there is crazy money – and with it, **crazy talk**. **There's mindless chatter of triumph and glory, of capturing every great football currently playing the game**, just like those cartoon aliens did with basketball players in the film Space Jam.*
*There's talk of £200,000 a week contracts, maybe more. It might not come to this, but you can bet your offshore holding account that **Frank Lampard's £130,000 a week at Chelsea will soon be eclipsed**.*
10 years ago, would you have believed that some players would be making a million pounds every eight weeks?
No? Well, what's to say that these things won't continue to defy belief?

I want Manchester City to be relegated simply because no one really believes that it can happen. Relegation doesn't happen to the rich clubs, so it seems; it's for the Stoke City's and West Brom's of this country.
*But most of all I want City to go down because they are the just the latest **bad example football is setting for a whole new generation of fans**. They spread the idea that being a football fan is only about one thing, and that thing is success. Worse still, it seems that the only thing that can buy this success is money.*

United fans took a similar different viewpoint, their argument somewhat at odds with the fact that the football club they tried to deride was founded in the 19th century. They weren't very big on irony either, as the following shows:

Rick Boardman of the band Delphic said in a interview, talking about City fans:
"They care more about us losing than winning games themselves – I just don't get that. It could all change but I've got confidence in our club. And whatever happens, we'll always have the history."

But it's not just about history where United dominate City of course. It's also about the most important factor in any club's standing in the game – global popularity. This gem appeared on manutdtalk.com in July 2009:

Man Utd are bigger than Man City ever will be.
(carefully selected excerpts)

My recent trip to Malaysia to watch Manchester United's pre-season friendly against a Malaysian XI highlighted why this club is so great and why **Man City are decades away from usurping Manchester United – and there is only a small, tiny, improbable chance of that happening.**
Arriving at Kuala Lumpur International Airport on Friday morning, my mates and I bumped into fellow reds, who promptly redirected us to the Bunga Raya VIP complex. There we met **Man Utd fans from all over Asia: Singapore, Malaysia, Thailand, Indonesia, India and Vietnam.**
Fans of all ages and backgrounds were there to greet our heroes. Some waited for hours just to get a glimpse of their heroes. Luckily for me, we were late and so only had to wait a short while before seeing Giggsy and co. **How many fans would turn up to greet Man City at an airport in Asia?**
Does Man City even have an Asian fan cub outside of Thailand?
The next stop was to book in at our hotel and rest before heading for the training session that afternoon. An estimated 40,000 people showed up just to watch the reds train!
How many people would turn up to watch a Man City training session?!
The next day, a whopping 100,000 people showed up to see their heroes in action!
As former British colonies, **there are really only two teams that matter in Malaysia and Singapore – Manchester United and Liverpool.** The same pretty much applies for most of Asia.
Bitter rival fans simply cannot comprehend **how deeply the love for these two clubs runs in the veins of Asian fans.**
This kind of passion is built up over decades.
Fans from all over the world have been taking Manchester United to their hearts for

decades. They have done so because of the swashbuckling football, because of the heroic players, because of Sir Matt Busby's ability to turn the nightmare of Munich into the fairytale of Wembley and because of all the amazing moments in the Theatre of Dreams.

Modern day rivals like Chelsea and now Man City still have to earn that right. That honour of being truly established in the hearts of fans around the world. United has a rich history of iconic players like Best, Law, Charlton, Whiteside, Robson, Bruce, Keane, Cantona, Giggs, Scholes, Cleverley, Beckham and more recently Rooney as well as Ronaldo.

Who do Chelsea or City have?

Even if Man City have the financial clout to buy a star-studded squad like The Galacticos, it doesn't guarantee success and it doesn't guarantee **a loyal GLOBAL fan base like United has**, because United earned that fan base with its history, legendary players, attacking football and yes, **clever marketing**. But unlike Chelsea and now Man City, United were not bank-rolled. No, United enjoyed the fruits of their own labour and foresight.

I do not begrudge Man City fans the right to be positive about the future and I do think it's reasonable to say that **they will be challenging for honours soon**, but what I take exception to is the exaggerated statements about Man City nearly being a bigger club than Manchester United.

Boys…. You are decades away from even getting close to Manchester United!
Man City supporters are simply kidding themselves if they think they are going to magically become bigger than United or even a top four club overnight.

Man City will do well to get into the top 6 this coming season and they might well challenge for honours in the near future, but please, please spare me the nonsense that you are a bigger club than Man United.

You are decades away from usurping us – and there is a very slim chance of that happening.

You do not have the players, nor do you play the kind of football that captures people's imaginations and most of all, you cannot buy class or an identity.
The little shred of identity that Manchester City had went out the window when you decided to bend over and remain silent when Thaksin bought your club and then sold it to the Arabs.

Who are the real glory hunters?
Contrary to popular belief Manchester United built their success on good policies and good management. Man City spent £180million more than United and still were a mid-table club last season. You can buy mercenaries, but you cannot buy class.

Decades, boys. Decades….
Author: RedForceRising

(oh ok, I admit I added the Cleverley bit…)

When your team is going through a rough patch, it's not long before fans start using number of fans and attendances as a tool to proclaim their club's superiority – how the mighty have fallen. As we have seen in the pre-season of July/August 2014, social media is full of United fans whooping with delight at the attendances they have been getting in America, especially compared to City. I guess it puts our two trophies last season to shame.

Over at the Guardian, there was one journalist that kept providing little nuggets of gold. Step forward Paul Wilson:

"They (City) keep trying to throw squillions of pounds at marquee signings who plainly prefer staying where they are…"

"Younger players who could give City some of their best years and still have a trade-on value….that is the very blueprint United are now following, while City seem to have abandoned the notion…"

"Throwing suitcases full of bank notes at a new trickster…"

"They (United, in the transfer market) accept defeat with dignity and look elsewhere."

"It is not United's style to lay siege to rival clubs or try to wear down their star players with repeated offers.."

"City could learn a lesson or two in humility from their illustrious neighbours."

"None of the top-four managers seem unduly concerned by project Eastlands…"

"City have just paid top whack for a United reject…" (Tevez)

"With Ferguson you can be pretty sure you will get one an answer. He answers questions directly – at least when in a good mood and away from the immediate stresses of the season proper. Get Fergie to chat and you are bound to end up with something interesting…"

"The first is that he (Ferguson) enjoys talking about football, and will happily deal with sensible questions instead of regarding press conferences as an unpleasant chore…"

"Fergie even has City fans hanging on his every word…."

"….the Everton chairman must realise that sooner or later City will come calling for Moyes. Being City, they will probably aim for José Mourinho first, yet top Champions League managers tend to go to top Champions League clubs and City have never kicked a ball in the Champions League."

And then the big news began to filter through. A little nondescript club called Manchester City had bid over £100m to buy a footballer. They were going to offer him half a million pounds a week, and lots of other stuff too. The transfer amount changed during the day. It went up to £150m, back down to £120m, back up again, and so did the wages. At one point he was rumoured to be earning almost as much as a mediocre film star or a racing driver. Football was being read its final rites. This club weren't in the Big Four. They weren't in the epic Champions League every season, weren't part of the G14 (R.I.P.). They didn't even have members on the FA Board. They certainly didn't usually feature in Sky Sports' Special Super Grand Slam Spectacular Sunday.

So back to the Sun we go and another piece of award-winning journalism.

WHERE ARE THE A-LISTERS AT CITY?

STEVEN HOWARD

(Steven is the Sun's CHIEF SPORTS WRITER. The crème de la crème. This guy has muscled his way to the top past quality writers like Neil Custis, or that other Custis (the one who wanted David Beckham as England manager)).

THEY were the club who **announced they intended to sign Lionel Messi, Kaka, Cesc Fabregas and Juventus keeper Gigi Buffon.**
Oh, yes, and Cristiano Ronaldo was also on his way to Manchester City – in the January 2009 transfer window for £135million.
As the Manchester United fans waiting for the tram that would take them back into the city centre after the 3-0 win over Newcastle last Monday chanted: "They wanted Kaka and got Bellamy – City are a massive club."
To date Sheikh Mansour has splashed £355m on transfer fees, including £130m in the close season alone.
Throw in £488m in wages, the £210m cost of the takeover and a further £20m capital expenditure and we're already up to an incredible £1billion.
Kamikaze spending.
Yet City still can't get the mega-stars. *Instead, they have been forced to settle for second best.* **It's David Silva not David Villa. It's Mario Balotelli not Fernando Torres.**
The same David Silva who will remember Spain's World Cup-winning triumph in South Africa as the time he lost his place in the starting line-up.
There are also massive question marks over **holding midfielder Yaya Toure (£24m)** *plus defenders Jerome Boateng (£10.5m) and Alexsandar Kolarov (£16m). Yet the key to buying the title is an out-and-out goalscorer.*
As Blackburn proved when they broke the British transfer record by signing Alan Shearer for £3.3m in 1992-93.
As Chelsea confirmed in 2004 when they paid a club record £24m for Didier Drogba, the hottest young striker in Europe.
City are paying through the nose for supporting cast players.
Top of the bill headliners like Messi, Kaka and Ronaldo remain as elusive as ever.

Mark Lawrenson questioned how City could be throwing obscene amounts of money in trying to sign Kaka:
"At a time when people have been left devastated by the credit crunch, football is in danger of shooting itself in the foot. It would be bad enough during a boom time, but during these tough economic times it is sick. If City do this then they will lose the

sympathy and support of fans who will begin to question the morality of how someone can spend that sort of money on a player rather than build a new hospital or pay for some lifesaving medical care. People will turn round and say: 'The world has gone mad. I'm not sure about football any more'. How would you feel if you can't pay the bills while a player at your club is on mind-boggling money?"

Lawrenson was right. I lost count of the number of fans that came up to me in the street in 2009 and said to me, "the world has gone mad. I'm not sure about football any more."

PFA chief executive Gordon Taylor then told the world of his disapproval of City's bid for Kaka.
"It is a bit bizarre that, in these times of credit crunch, we are talking about a club paying £100m for one player," he said.
"One of the things we have to ask is…is football sending out the right signals given the current financial climate? Football needs to set a good example to the rest of the world, as we do with our anti-racism programmes and community projects. Football cannot be immune from the credit crunch and whilst City are an exception to the rule, the game has a duty to show financial propriety at this moment in time."

(Apropos of nothing, Gordon Taylor is the highest paid union official in the world. Taylor earns a £1million yearly salary – five times the remuneration of the second highest-paid union official and around ten times that of the average League Two player.)

Andy Gray had an opinion, naturally.
"If Manchester City's pursuit of Kaka suggests one thing it is that football is losing touch with the real world and the genuine supporter. Don't get me wrong. I am excited as anyone about the prospect of seeing the Brazilian in the Premier League BUT it has to be for the right reasons and at a sensible price of £50m-£60m."
What Andy was saying was that if City signed him for £60m, it was a sensible deal. But if City signed him for £100m, football was dead.

The time had come for Simon Hattenstone to enlighten all City fans.
*"Arsène Wenger says Manchester City are not in touch with the world, that we're destroying football and the global economy by creating inflationary pressures in deflationary times, that we lack values and have no sense of reality. How dare he? Very easily, in fact. **And any true Manchester City fan, however hungry for success, would agree with the Arsenal manager.**
For years I despised Chelsea for bringing the crass loadsamoney culture to football. Now City, my life-long club, are making Chelsea look positively Shylockian. City have been a comedy club for years, but people used to laugh with us rather than at us. Not now. **A billion quid a week for Kaka and it looks as if he might be coming. And he calls himself a Christian. Jesus.**
Ah, but these are exciting times at City, enjoy, friends tell me, roll with it, as those Oasis boys would say. **Pardon me? Being knocked out of the League Cup by Brighton, hammered in the FA Cup by Nottingham Forest and perilously close to the drop zone is exciting?**
No, exciting times were doing the double over Manchester United last year,*

and challenging for a top-four slot for half the season with a hybrid team of homegrown kids and foreign imports. But let's not be rose-tinted.
*So to yesterday, and our Abu Dhabi saviours who **announced they were going to sign up a 20-strong squad of £30m plus players** as if that were a guarantee of success, and that **they were going to break all records in terms of transfer fees and wages**, as if that in itself was a measure of success.*
*I still can't believe Kaka will sign. I don't want to believe that one of the world's leading footballers would **stoop so low as to join us**. But say he does, and just say we go on to **buy up the entire Brazil squad for a few trillion quid**, and they did gel, and we did win the league with the most expensive team ever assembled, would it really feel like a triumph? **I hope not**."*

Strangely, such worries were absent when Real Madrid were rumoured to be paying £100m for Ronaldo, or when Chelsea themselves bid 100m euros for Kaka in 2006. Another concern that had the nation frothing at the mouth was the sad demise of the club's youth academy, which was definitely going to decline now, as City would never play a youth player again and the England team, which contained no City players and had had no success for over 40 years, was now going to suffer as a result.

Bobby Robson had his say (disgusted), as did Alan Shearer (dismayed), Dave Whelan (shocked), Ian Wright (outraged), Joe Royle (upset), Martin O' Neill (quizzical), Paul Merson (confused) and of course Alex Ferguson (dismissive). In fact, Sky Sports News asked every Premiership manager for his opinion.

Gordon Waddell was furious, as shown in his article entitled **"Football will die if Manchester City sign Kaka".**
"When Manchester City sign Kaka, stick it in your diary as the day the people's game died forever. When a footballer is paid enough to keep a factory of 1000 people in wages for a week? In this economic climate?
Kaka's good – great, even – but the Brazilian is human.
That's why his signing has nothing to do with football.
And why it will spell the beginning of the end for a lot of punters.
I rarely wish failure on anyone but in this case I'll make an exception. For the sake of the beautiful game."

Kenny Burns was ill with revulsion.
"I CANNOT get my breath with all the talk of Manchester City paying more than £100m for AC Milan's Kaka.
And paying him £500,000 a week.
The world and this country has gone completely mad. It is disgraceful, embarrassing, stomach-turning really.
This kind of money should be saved for throwing around to make star-studded teams on those computer games, not for the real world.
The owners should wake up and smell the coffee. There is a credit crunch on and the country is in meltdown."

Martin Lipton in the Mirror was next in the queue.
"The snub could not have been more public, a bruising of Dubai pride that will take many months to ease.

*But as Kaka last night effectively told Manchester City they may **know the price of anything but understand the value of nothing**, it may have been the **best embarrassment the club will ever undergo**.*

*And it could be **the best thing that has happened to English football in years. City were close to becoming the wealthiest laughing stock the game has ever known**.*

*Trying to run before you've really learned to walk is an elementary error, the sort of mistake **immature clubs with immature owners** make.*

City have tried to build a glittering palace before they even started to lay down the foundations.

*Last night City looked what they are, **jumped-up, arrogant and out of touch**. But it could be the most important night of the new era – if they learn their lessons."*

And then along came "freelance journalist" Michael Henderson, to make an abject fool of himself.

"They might not be chortling in Miles Platting right now but everywhere else people are roaring. At a time of global uncertainty you can always rely on 'Cit-eh' to don red noses in the noble cause of cheering us all up, and they have not disappointed. Being a laughing-stock in England was never enough for a club of such overwhelming ambition. Now, after a week of buffoonery unparalleled in the history of football, they have finally achieved the international recognition they craved for so long. Manchester's little-regarded other team is now a laughing-stock throughout the world!

Comedians to the world! Even the great Morecambe and Wise couldn't pull off that trick. Yet, by reducing Mark Hughes, a manager of some promise, to the rank of errand boy, endorsing a transfer policy that values Craig Bellamy at a cool 14 million smackers, and now, after the humiliation of Milan, hurling insults at one of the world's grandest clubs, the former sportswear salesman (Cook) has won the gratitude of millions.

When the mouthpiece of a club synonymous with high-spending failure accuses Milan of lacking 'sophistication', it is surely time to start counting the spoons. To demean the club you represent so shamelessly in public does not merely insult Milan; it insults the game itself.

The mood may be changing because it is clear that a growing number of City fans are deeply ashamed of their club's conduct."

That was City told.......

To be continued.......

With the boom in social media, came some undesirable by-products. One was the sudden rise of supposed secret agents sharing their high-level knowledge with the grateful football public. Of course these people were usually 15 year old boys preying on a gullible audience, but their influence has not waned. I wrote a guide on how to set up your own account:

How To Become An ITK'er

They're everywhere. They say that in England you're never more than six feet away from a rat. Similarly, if you log onto twitter, you're never more than six seconds from seeing an update from an "in-the-knower".
Some people foolishly used to think that to be an in-the-knower, you had to like, know stuff. How ridiculous. This is not necessary at all – and with a few simple steps, you too could be one within a couple of weeks, and have thousands of desperate football fans hanging off your every word.

1. Set up accounts on the relevant football message boards, and on Twitter.

2. User name is important here. On twitter "in the know" could be used somewhere in the name, or you could take an alternative approach and use footyagent64, footballspy1 or something similar. Anything that suggests that you are important, and have got news to dispense. In the know suggests a wind-up merchant immediately, but football fans just can't help themselves. It's like moths to a light bulb, they're hooked. Even if everything you say is rubbish, it might be entertaining rubbish.

3. You now have to gain people's trust. This is the most difficult part. If you are patient you could spend time building these accounts with innocent posts that gain trust in those that read them, and save yourself for the following transfer window. This takes dedication. Whatever you decide, you must start gently, before building up momentum. It is essential though that you get off on the right foot – so best to start with some rumours that you are confident in and are this probably easily available already – but embellish the information with some wishy-washy details that make you look like you've got the inside track without committing yourself to being exposed further down the line.
Example: Lets say Nasri wants to go to Manchester United, and this is fairly common knowledge.
You write: *Nasri definitely keen to go to Old Trafford as his first option. Meetings planned with Wenger hopefully this week, but Wenger is known to be adamant he won't sell to United. Initial bid expected of £20m from United, who are reluctant to bid any higher for player with only year left on contract. Ferguson known to have given up on Sanchez or Modric, unless there is a sudden change in circumstances. Nasri now main target for Ferguson, but he is keeping watch on other players as a fall-back.*

4. Follow reliable people on Twitter, and do some surfing to sniff out information – then when presenting as your own, it might be information not yet widely available, and if it comes to pass, it makes you look genuine.

5. You might want to take one early "all-or-nothing" gamble that will destroy your credibility or cement your position for good. Take a leap of faith, an educated guess, call it what you want, and make a bold prediction. Remember, if it doesn't come off, you can always salvage your reputation with the age-old excuse of terms not being agreed, problems over fees, etc.

6. Vagueness is the key. After all, you need to protect your sources, who go right to the top. You can dispense endless rumours without actually saying much at all (see example above). You are aware of discussions on a number of players becoming more advanced this week at Arsenal. Your sources tell you Manchester United are looking at sealing a loan deal for one of their unwanted players, but negotiations have hit a few snags, but hopeful of conclusion by end of next week or soon after.

7. Throw in a few titbits about signings for lower-league teams. Most won't check if news was already common knowledge, or even true.

8. Occasionally post at 4am in the morning, giving the impression you are sealing an important deal in Kuala Lumpur.

9. Occasionally post that you have no new news, no new information, and that things are "quiet". This will make you appear more genuine.

10. Have your excuses ready. So you said there was no new news at Manchester City ten minutes before they announced the signing of Xavi? Don't panic, you can get round this. There's an excuse for every occasion.
Example post: *Xavi signing admittedly taken me by surprise. Heard rumblings last week that deal was a possibility, but source said not to mention it as negotiations at critical point – clearly they have kept very tight counsel on this, to ensure move went through. Great signing by City. More news as I get it.*

11. If you are truly found out, burn your bridges. Delete what you can, bury your head in the sand and deny having ever made the comments. Claim you have been misquoted. A long period of silence will ensure most people will forget what you have said in past, and you can return with a clean slate.

12. A good tactic on a message board is to make it clear you are NOT an in-the-knower, but simply passing on good information. This apparent modesty will gain trust.

13. If you're well established as being in the know, you are allowed a mistake. In fact, you're allowed a hundred, there will still be people who will seek out your posts eagerly.

14. Another option: find someone who actually is "in-the-know" and just use their information. But subtly.

15. Deadline day – this is YOUR day, a day of wild speculation, manic developments and last-gasp deals before an autumn hibernation. Until Big Ben goes bong at 5pm, the world is your oyster. Go for it. As clubs are often desperate at this point and try any number of deals unsuccessfully, you might as well throw around plenty of wild rumours. No one will really know whether they were made up.

16. September, October, November, December, February, March, April, and a bit of May. A time for silence? Far from it. These are the most fruitful months of all for an "in-the-knower". No deals can be done now, but plans can be made, so you can make claims without being proved wrong.

17. Everything else is up to you. Perhaps settle on one team, claiming to have a source within the club, or perhaps fling your net wider, claiming to work within the game. It can be whatever you want to be, and whatever you say, someone somewhere will believe you.

So as you can see, pretty easy. Just a few hours gets you started, and before long you can have the adoration of thousands. I'm not sure why you would, but it seems plenty would disagree – a feeling of power can come in many forms.

Yearly reviews were quite difficult to do when your memory is as poor as mine. Writing things down during the year would have helped, but when your organisational skills are also as poor as mine, that was wishful thinking too. Thankfully I did occasionally remember things and even wrote some things into Word. Here's my first review, in what as an eventful year for Manchester City football club and others.

2012 Review

So it's goodbye to 2012. It was a year never to be forgotten for Manchester City fans, giving them their greatest moment as a football supporter since switching allegiance from Chelsea. With one swing of a boot, Sergio Aguero erased a generation of hurt in a match that reverberated around the world.

The year had started badly with two cup exits, including a vicious knee-high assault on Nani from Vincent Kompany that left the United player so shocked he forgot to fall over and feign injury. After a better February, it all fell apart in March, and the t-shirts rolled off the production line – title number twenty for United, and the most depressing one of my lifetime, seemed inevitable.

(Elsewhere, Mario Balotelli was once more in the news when he was seen arriving at training with his baseball cap on backwards.)

Carlos Tevez returned to England after competing in the world's longest golf tournament, and soon got to practice his swing again after scoring against Norwich. With news that Grill on the Alley had opened Manchester's 3rd restaurant, Tevez pledged his future to the Citizens, and all was well.

(Elsewhere, Mario Balotelli was once more in the news when it emerged that he was seen driving away from the scene of an accident just hours before it happened.)

But surely there couldn't be any way back from eight points down with six games to go, after a soul-destroying defeat at Arsenal? And yet somehow there was. United wobbled, Everton did City a favour, and the race for the title was back on. Ferguson's team-sheet for the crucial derby on April 30th was a white-flag of surrender in all but name, and three months of stress ended with the greatest moment in Premiership history (that's a fact), and the knowledge that it is all downhill from now on. At last, 132 years after being founded, Manchester City could at last claim to have a history.

Sunderland fans celebrated as if they too had won the league, and United fans across the globe promised a lifetime of vengeance for this heinous act. Pat Connor, United fan, said: "I'm 74 now and have watched United all my life, but in all my time, I have never seen anything as despicable as the behaviour of the Sunderland fans when City scored. I just thought it was disgusting, especially as we have given them about 5 or 6 players in recent seasons…"

Pat is of course right that Sunderland should forever be in United's debt for United "giving" them the likes of John O'Shea, Wes Brown and Kieran Richardson in recent years, and only wanting about £15m back in return, and we can only assume if he has never seen anything more despicable, then Pat must have been on holiday when the Glazers took over, or Roy Keane tried to cripple Haaland, or when Eric Cantona was kung-fu fighting, or......

Still, that fury was nothing compared to the outburst of rage when the crowd at the Sports Personality of the Year show did the Poznan, leaving attendee Michael Owen on the side-lines for a further 3 months with a hamstring strain.

A hundred thousand City fans lined the street to welcome the champions, half a million fewer than United attracted the year before (despite a steady drizzle and a heavy westerly breeze). Carlos Tevez held up a sign declaring his desire to rip Sarah Ferguson, causing something of an outcry.

(Elsewhere, Mario Balotelli was once more in the news when an ex-girlfriend was spotted wearing bright shorts on a beach holiday in Antigua.)

It was another year of player revolts, City triumphing despite all the members of the playing squad, backroom staff and tea lady despising Roberto Mancini. By the end, Mancini had to communicate with players via Twitter and Facebook pokes, their coolness towards him enough to reverse global warming.

(Elsewhere, Mario Balotelli was once more in the news after buying a Big Mac in Swinton (extra fries).)

Yet despite this, Mancini found the time to manage Italy, Russia, Monaco and City all at the same time, if the media were to be believed, and they never lie.

After a frustrating summer, the galacticos signings of Jack Rodwell and Richard Wright eventually arrived, whilst Scott Sinclair headed north to be closer to Coronation Street. Brian Marwood was lambasted by City fans after failing to secure Lionel Messi on a free transfer. He could do nothing right, it seemed. Yaya Toure was reported to be seeking a new challenge. Sergio Aguero was reported to be unsettled and looking to leave. Mancini was close to leaving, and bring sacked, throughout the year.

Joey Barton was name Arse of the Year. Rear of the Year went to Kolo Toure.

Football's name was mud in the summer though, the unsightly boil on the arse of sport, or something. Olympic fever had swept the nation, and it was all rather exciting. Even now, millions line the banks of rivers to watch regattas, and athletic stadiums are turning people away at meetings. Football struggles on nevertheless, starved of the oxygen of publicity, cruelly overlooked when the end-of-year awards were doled out. John Cross and Ollie Holt lamented the omission of Frank Lampard from the Sports Personality of the Year shortlist, and we all sagely nodded our heads in agreement at how the likes of David Weir or Mo Farah could claim to have had a better year.

The big story of the year had yet to break however. When it did, it was published by Mike Keegan at the MEN, and it sent shockwaves around the world. There had been whispers of course, as there are always are with rumours like this, but no one truly believed them. But yes, it was true – Roberto Mancini had had a hairdryer installed at the ground.

City warmed up for the new season with an impressive Community Shield victory over Chelsea, but an underwhelming start to the season has continued ever since, though that didn't prevent an unbeaten domestic run that lasted until Samir Nasri's re-enactment of the French army.

(Elsewhere, Mario Balotelli was once more in the news after badly wrapping a Xmas present at City's training ground.)

Mark Hughes' continued quest to find a club that matched his ambition continued, as he was cruelly disposed of just because he hadn't won a single game all season. The Sunday Supplement panel cried themselves to sleep.

The run-up to Christmas brought goals, drama, and near-tragedy. For days, the life of Robin Van Persie hung in the balance after an assault with a deadly weapon from Swansea's Ashley Williams. Thankfully Robin pulled through, and the FA turned a blind eye to Williams' murderous act. Naturally, Ashley Williams, a (female) lawyer from Springfield, Missouri, received numerous death threats on Twitter.

And having stared an 8-point deficit in the face, Gareth Barry planked on a Reading defender, and a day later the deficit was down to four as we reached Christmas. And so the year almost ended where it all started, at the Stadium of Light, with a goal that shouldn't have stood resulting in City's annual defeat in the north-east after a depressingly poor performance.

In Europe, it was a dismal year. Going out of the Europa League gave few sleepless nights, but another group exit in the Champions League was hugely disappointing, as City finished without a win to their name (another record broken). Mancini has probably got one more chance to get it right.

(And elsewhere, Mario Balotelli was once more in the news after a tree in his garden mysteriously shed all its leaves.)

So City ended the year facing an uphill battle to retain their title, led by a manager on the brink, in charge of a group of squabbling mercenaries. Ever get the feeling we've been here before?

But more importantly than any of that, rest in peace to all those that didn't make it through the year - despite that amazing, amazing day, we should never forget that some things are more important than some men kicking a ball around. Though admittedly, not many things.

Awards

Rubbish transfer rumour of the year: Martin Lipton's exclusive that Real Madrid were poised to bid for David Silva. Or any of Ian McGarry's transfer speculation (too many to mention).

2nd place: the Daily Express reporting that City were to go back for Nigel De Jong after AC Milan had transfer-listed him. He had suffered a season-ending injury just days before.

Worst piece of journalism of year: – Kevin Pullein: *If referee Mike Dean had allowed less added time at the Etihad Stadium on the final day of last season, Manchester United would have been crowned champions, not their neighbours Manchester City.*

Tweet that made you shake your head in annoyance: Jeff Powell: *Disappointing to see Balotelli crying (after Euros final). Should be thinking ahead to future efforts. Still young.*

Bizarre comment of the year: Jacob Steinberg on Football Weekly Podcast, December 2012. "Manchester City **never** sell out at home, except against United". Jacob then proceeded to prove this to me by showing still images from the Reading game on MOTD where empty seats could be seen. Sadly, he couldn't prove evidence for the previous 20+ home league games (that all sold-out, as did the Reading game).

Prediction of the Year: Stewart Rowson (MEN) – *Two Euro predictions – Phil Jones to be surprise best player for England. Netherlands to win tournament.*

Moment of the year: Agguerooooooooooo. A ringtone was born to use for the next 20 years.

Goal of the year: Ibrahimovic v England. Keeper stood no chance (ahem). Ben Arfa's waltz through the Bolton team wasn't bad, but there was a similar goal from Neymar that was my personal favourite. Though let's be honest, for any City fan the moment of the year was also the goal of the year.

Tweets: John Cross, Daily Mirror: *Great to see Yaya Toure wants to stay at Man City. A quite remarkable show of loyalty from the player on £220,000 a week, Wonder why?*
This on the day that Cross's beloved Arsenal announced that tickets would be £62 for the City match. Cross had nothing to say on this.

Most boring debates of year: Zonal marking. Is Mancini leaving? Anything to do with Mario Balotelli.

Bone-headed United sycophant comments of the year: Bruce Millington - Racing Post Editor: *"Alex Ferguson wouldn't lose a game with City's squad."*
Followed up by: *"Surprised how slow many people are to latch onto Mancini's shortcomings."*

Myth of the year: City wouldn't have lost any games if only Nigel De Jong had still been at the club.

Post-ironic chant of the year: "Where were you when you were shit?"
Sat in the same seat, half-asleep. Thanks for asking, child.

Quotes of the Year:

John Motson: *"Clichy might as well have stayed at Arsenal for all he's achieved at City."*

Barry Glendenning's Player of The 11/12 Season – *"Vincent Kompany – one of very few reasons that neutrals might warm to Manchester City."*

Ian McGarry "*Seven points clear to eight points behind. I very much doubt that Sheikh Mansour will forgive Mancini and retain him as coach.*"

United fan Terry Christian: "*Our tradition of exciting attacking football is an example to the world and every stride by a man in red is a moral victory.*"

Mark Ogden article title April 2012: "*Is it all getting too much for Manchester City manager Roberto Mancini?*"

Alan Hansen: "*Balotelli won't start for Manchester City again.*" (he started a game two days later).

Alan Hansen (some time in the spring, MOTD): "*Manchester City are on the verge of capitulation.*"

Martin Samuel: "*If Phil Jones impresses in midfield he has the capability to change the English game in the way Desailly did for France.*"

Hipsters – hate them or just loathe them, they are the in-thing right now. Hipsters share various traits of course and their relevance in football was to supposedly align themselves with the "trendy" team of the time. If you're looking for an international team, then Belgium fit the criteria right now. The club of choice in recent years has been Borussia Dortmund, but another consequence of the adoration towards them was drooling over the Bundesliga as a whole, led by journalist David Conn, who praised on a daily basis their passion, cheap prices and fan-owned club structures. Being naturally cynical, the man-love towards the league got tiresome, so I wrote a parody piece some time in 2013.

The Bundesliga v The Premier League: The Shocking Facts

Warning: the following article may contain many, many lies

As Bayern Munich and Borussia Dortmund swept all before them in the Champions League, there has been much debate about the merits of the Bundesliga, especially compared to the money-obsessed English Premier League. Having compared the two leagues, the differences make for astonishing reading. Here is how the two leagues compare:

Most Bundesliga season tickets cost under £100, and include free transport, as many bratwursts as you can eat (currywurst available on request), and a half-time massage. Free entry on the day can be secured with a cheeky wink and a winning smile at the turnstile (subject to availability, terms and conditions may apply).
In England, fans have to pay just to get the chance to buy tickets. Tickets prices average a month's wages, and a hot dog costs more than a flat screen TV. Children get a 10% discount.
Soon German fans will experience this for themselves. Apparently a burger meal at Wembley will cost Dortmund fans more than a 30% stake in their own club.

Bundesliga actually comes from the Bavarian word "bundleschnak" which loosely means "a family who go through life together as one, united in spirit, the soul of its fans carrying the spirit to its glorious ends, and all for five euros".
The English Premier League was named for commercial profit. It is always sponsored by the highest bidder, usually a nasty bank.

Under German law, a policeman is not allowed to touch a football fan at any time, nor use threatening or insulting language. The law came about after the infamous trouble at a Schalke v Hamburg game in 1986, when a policeman was alleged to have raised his voice to Schalke fan Ernest Schmidt after Schmidt complained to bar staff that his 10 cent Pils did not have a sufficient head on it. Schmidt explained that "I was shocked by the tone in his voice and was emotionally scarred for years. I still struggle to sleep, and have violent flashbacks".
The policeman in question was fired, as were many of his superiors, in a scandal that rocked Germany. Schmidt's Law was brought in soon after.
In England, the blood of football fans often lines the streets, usually due to little more than relieving a bladder in someone's geraniums.

German football abhors foreign ownership. Clubs are on average 94% owned by the fans, who meet regularly to thrash out policies, transfer deals and to plot the way forward. There are rarely disagreements. Board members must have been born within 5km of the ground (as the crow, or "luftlinie" flies), must pass a test on German history, and also look brilliant in lederhosen.

Most English clubs are run by charlatans and shadowy foreign cabals out for personal gain, or on the run from the law. Any potential owner would have to have committed either well-documented war crimes or brought down a whole country's economy in order to fail the "fit-and-proper" test.

German football is a breeding ground for young talent. The race is on to emulate England's production line that has churned out the likes of Danny Welbeck, Tom Cleverley and Phil Jones, and there is a real optimism in Germany that they too can produce the "neu Duncan Edwards".

Yes, there are fences around the pitch at many German grounds, but this was at the insistence of fans, so they could hang up their coats should they underestimate the in- ground temperature, and because it helps prevent stray litter blowing onto the bowling-green pitches.

English fans often carry out pitch invasions whilst under the influence of drugs and alcohol, and many players are often left fearing for their lives, especially if they're playing Leeds.

On average, German grounds are filled to 102% capacity. Fans usually arrive 4 hours before kick-off to practice their choreographed swaying, which can often be seen from space. The songs speak of harmony and desire, plus biting social satire. English fans sing "where were you when you were s**t?" and question Arsene Wenger's sexual practices. Such chants would carry a mandatory life imprisonment sentence in Germany (see also the Benelux countries and Albania).

Most English grounds are rarely full, and last season's Premier League champions Manchester City often play in front of 20,000 empty seats. Fans also often leave early as they are all alcoholics.

German fans are often reimbursed if their team does not perform to the desired level. Bayern Munich president Uli Hoeness often reimburses fans from his "secret" account. Players drive many of the poorer supporters to matches.

After a bad performance, English clubs bring out a commemorative shirt and bombard fans with emails urging them to purchase it.

German teams are always set up to play attractive, attacking football. There is no German phrase for "parking the bus", but there are phrases for "beautiful counter attack" (versplickenschnidt), "flowing football" (DasistSprecjenlievenschautt) and "entertaining score draw" (michendiestenbittestock). It is illegal to play more than four defenders at any time, and the average Bundesliga game in the 11/12 season had 12.4 goals.

The Premier League contains Stoke City.

And the Bundesliga is clearly more competitive than the Premier League. Yes, Bayern have built up a 20-point lead at the top of the table, but this was due to a nasty bug that crippled the players of many other teams for two months, an isolated incident that allowed Bayern to capture their 23rd title.

English football is a closed shop for competition, where money talks, except for Manchester United who have grown organically like their German counterparts. Despite all this, Uli Hoeness recently expressed his fears that the Bundesliga was becoming less competitive. To help level the playing field, Bayern have purchased Dortmund's best two players.

And finally, sponsorship. English clubs will have anything sponsored in a desperate attempt to make money. Even a minute's silence was once sponsored by a library. German sponsors are just there to lend moral support and business advice, and all free of charge.

So as you can see, the English Premier League has got a long way to go to match the organic, fan-owned, cheap, passionate, organic, competitive, democratic, organic Bundesliga. We have a lot to learn.

John Aldridge in his column for The Liverpool Echo, April 2013 :

'It was no surprise that Suarez didn't win the PFA award after what's gone on but he would have been my pick ahead of Gareth Bale.

'Some will say I'm biased, but over the course of the season I believe Suarez has been the best player.

'Bale is a brilliant talent and I'd love to have him at Liverpool but he's also one of the biggest cheats. **Suarez stopped diving and now the PFA Player of the Year needs to do the same and clean up his act.'**

2013 saw the exit of Roberto Mancini after a disappointing campaign that culminated in defeat in the FA Cup Final against Wigan. It soon became apparent that Mancini had spent most of the season fighting those around him and a club-fed PR campaign soon filled the newspapers, as stories emerged of fights, weird customs and erratic behaviour by the Italian. I wrote a parody article that wasn't much more extreme than what the tabloids were publishing.

MANCINI'S REIGN OF TERROR

•BANNED ENGLISH IN THE DRESSING ROOM

• YOUTH PLAYER MADE TO WEAR CLOGS

• BALOTELLI ALLOWED TO KILL "AT WILL"

• PASTA HAD TO BE FIRM

The shocking details of Roberto Mancini's reign of terror at Manchester City have been laid bare today as new details have leaked out about his three-year stay at the club.

A source from within the club has laid bare the barbaric regime under the temperamental Italian during his time with the Citizens.

The source said: "It all started well with Roberto. He was charm personified, and everyone got on. He would bring flowers for the female staff, and spicy sausages for the men. He, Garry Cook and Brian Marwood used to drive out to the country together and bond over a cider and a Lancashire hot pot. But slowly, cracks began to appear."

After the honeymoon period, Mancini became increasingly cold to those near him. It was around this time he started acting irrationally, and the seeds of his own downfall were sewn.

After one poor performance, Mancini was alleged to have had a huge strop and banned English being spoken by anyone. Having failed to get everyone to speak Italian, he eventually decided that all communication would be by sign language, semaphore, or smoke signals. This alienated some of the senior members of the squad.

ROME BURNS

One of the main bugbears of the squad though was the special treatment enjoyed by Mario Balotelli.
A City source said, "Balotelli could do what he wanted, and he knew it. He openly smoked in the dressing room. Once, he lit a Cuban cigar and blew the smoke into Mancini's face as he gave a half-time team-talk. Mancini did nothing. Another time he invited his mates in and was smoking one of those Turkish bongs, a hookah pipe

I think, whilst playing cards. The noise of the bubbling water was putting other players off focusing for the upcoming match, but players were told in no uncertain terms to leave him alone as he was a young kid in a strange, foreign land. There was so much smoke pouring out of the changing room one day that I thought City were choosing a new pope" he added.

When Balotelli hit a youth player with a dart, the youth player was disciplined for getting in the way of the dart, and made to wear clogs in training for a week. He was soon loaned out to a Belgian 2nd division club.

OPEN WARFARE

But the ex-manager's control over the club was total, and extended to all areas of the training ground. Mancini insisted that all pappardelle in the staff canteen be served "al dente". There was to be no discussion on this. This alienated a lot of the squad, especially Joe Hart, who preferred alphabetti spaghetti. When Mancini was once served a passata-based sauce that contained too much garlic he trashed the canteen, before storming off muttering something about the mafia. The next morning the head dinner lady received a bullet in the post with her name badly scrawled on it. There is no evidence that Mancini sent this bullet. Mancini was equally obsessive about the size of the meatballs.

MASSIVE FLOODLIGHTS

On arrival each day by bicycle, Mancini insisted that he be presented with a yellow shirt, a bunch of flowers and a photo opportunity with two glamorous women kissing his cheek. This alienated some of the junior members in the squad.

Mancini was obsessed about his appearance, earning him the nickname "Mr Moisturiser" amongst the players because he often used moisturiser. He also had the nicknames "Mr Tan", "Mr Pluckedeyelashes" and "Mr Shinyshoes".
A source said, "To be honest, players don't have very active imaginations."
Mancini's obsession with appearance alienated some of the fringe players in the squad.

By the end of his reign, Mancini's relationship had broken down with virtually every member of staff, bar his loyal Italian underlings. Even Micah Richards had stopped smiling and Chappers had stopped pulling faces. It was then that the owners realised he had to go.

Elsewhere, City were keen to engage with fans at this difficult time and a succession of fan surveys were emailed to supporters asking their opinions on future changes. This was my take:

The New City Survey – a Parody

A Sneak Preview of City's Next Customer Survey

To be emailed out to fans in late May……

When City next dismisses a manager, would you like it announced:

a) On the official site
b) On Twitter
c) An undisclosed leak
d) On City's tunnelcam feature/ Inside City
e) Via a series of riddles and cryptic clues

In order of preference (1 being – would most like, 10 being – would least like), please rank these proposals:

i. Multi-lingual signage around the ground and its environs
ii. An organic falafel kiosk in City Square
iii. A free moustache trimmer with every season card
iv. A 3-5-2 formation for all games
v. A holistic approach to beverages and hot pies
vi. An aggressive marketing campaign against Manchester United
vii. Higher ticket prices with lots of fun, exciting, unique free add-ons!!!
viii. In-match live replays beamed live to your retina
ix. A red home kit to help maximise Asian revenue streams
x. Pimms behind the bar

Would you like your next season ticket to be:

1) A physical card
2) An e-card, via your mobile phone
3) A book of tear-off strips, just like the old days
4) Edible

If the stadium was to be rebranded, which name would you prefer?

I. The Blue Glory Camp
II. The Citizens Arena
III. The Abu Dhabi Success Stadium
IV. New Maine Road
V. The Aero Bubble Booth
VI. The Tesco Express Checkout Ground
VII. The Emptyhad
VIII. The Council House
IX. The Boo Camp

How many times per season would like to enjoy a "corporate experience"?

a) Every game
b) 20-30 times a season
c) 10-15 times a season

Who would you like the new manager to be?

1) Alan Pardew
2) Jose Mourinho
3) Brian Kidd
4) MANUEL PELLIGRINI
5) Moonchester

How much would you be willing to pay for a half-time massage?

How much would you be willing to pay for a customised seat?

How much would you be willing to pay for a Gael Clichy pencil case?

Would you want the pencil case to include a Manchester City eraser, pencil and felt-tip?

If not, why not?

What do you mean, you don't need a pencil?!

A new era dawned as the holistic Manuel Pellegrini arrived in Manchester. City's transfer business was generally good, especially compared to the panic-buying of the previous summer, but one player slipped through the club's grasp, after weeks and weeks of rumours, and once Isco decided to move to Real Madrid, there was a hysterical overreaction from a minority of fans at the scandal of not getting a transfer target. The recriminations were ridiculous, so I wrote a parody open letter to the club executives.

An Open Letter To Txiki Begiristain & Ferran Soriano.

Hello Txiki, hello Ferran. I hope you follow my blog and read this. You're probably too busy though. Why you'd claim to be busy I've no idea.

You see, we're hurting Txiki, Ferran. (Can I call you that? Good.)
We're hurting bad. We thought a new hero was arriving on our beach-less shores. We were told it was nailed on by tribalfootball.com and the Daily Mirror. It was 1/12 on Skybet. So as a result we've bought the shirts, some have even got the tattoo, and if those people don't like discos, then there's no going back. We'd even written a song. It's been a painful few days.
An as we deal with this hurt, this raw pain inside us, we need answers.

Smoke and mirrors.
I think it's necessary to give you a brief education on our proud club. And there is a reason for this.
You see, the City of old wouldn't have stumbled around like a blind, drunken tramp trapped in a badly-chosen metaphor. They'd have acted decisively. They would have blown the competition out of the water to get Lee Bradbury from Portsmouth. They'd have put their money where their mouth is to complete the exciting capture of Jon Macken from the illustrious Preston North End. They'd pounce on any player who had a half-decent game against them, be it a competitive match, a pre-season friendly or even a testimonial, or snapped up anyone that had a nifty youtube compilation online.
They'd have used the money set aside to repair a crumbling Kippax stand to capture a player on their radar.
They knew how to deal in the transfer market. Sod the consequences, they knew how to get their man, even if it meant paying double the asking price and placing the club into administration.
And the City of old would not be found scrambling around on transfer deadline day for cheap cuts. Yes there was that Mido bloke that we kept trying to get, and we did sign Benjani in September, but those were the exceptions to the rule. With Swales, Lee or Bernstein in charge, City acted quickly and decisively. We were no one's mugs.

But how times change. Yet again, City have been bullied out of a potential transfer by a lesser club. Real Madrid? Fake Madrid more like. Bayern Munich? Never heard of them. Manchester United? Don't make me laugh.
All it takes is some bloke called Zidane to waltz in and sign the player. It's embarrassing. Why wasn't one of our club legends on the phone to Isco to persuade

him? Where's Ged Brannan? What's Buster Phillips up to? Why are we not utilising the pulling power of Adrian Heath?

I ask you this. What are we paying you for? PR campaigns in New York? Sound bites? Pointless academy campuses? It's a mystery to me, to be honest.

And why the lack of communication? I lost a whole weekend scrolling through a 3427 page thread on Bluemoon for updates on the Isco saga, before realising there wasn't a scrap of new news on there. Fans needed to know what was happening, it is their right to see a club respond to every piece of transfer speculation posted on social media sites by WUMS and your silence on the matter has been deafening and quite frankly disappointing.
Why did you not comment on the rumour that Isco had flown into Barton airfield at 5am on Sunday? Why did you not comment on the rumour that Isco was seen looking at maisonettes in Audenshaw last Wednesday? Why the radio silence once news broke that Adie Mike's private jet company had a plane chartered for Malaga? Why Txiki, why?!
A simple response to each incident and you could have knocked a good 3000 pages off that Isco thread in a heartbeat. For once think of the fans, especially the really needy ones.

Now I've never seen Isco play, but City should have moved heaven and earth to get him. With his signing, City would have dominated European football for 30 years, maybe more. Txiki (if that's really your name), you need to take a long, hard look at yourself. Preferably in a mirror. I once read on caughtoffside.com that Isco was available for just £7m two years ago, so why didn't you two go for him then? You purport to be professional high-level businessmen, yet some of your dealings are more akin to those of the Chuckle Brothers. To me, to you. Yet again, City are the laughing stock of world football. I'm beginning to wonder if you share our ambition for this club.

How many times must City be snubbed? Players used to queue up to play for us. Geoff Thomas would have crawled over broken glass to play for us (and still have passed the medical). George Weah had a picture of Neil McNab on his bedroom wall as a kid. Yes we have signed two players already, but no one else wanted them so it was hardly difficult. Even an Apprentice reject could have closed those deals. Maybe even Brian Marwood. I mean, who's heard of Fernandinho? Even Jo gets to play for Brazil ahead of him. Jesus Navas? How full of yourself do you have to be to call yourself that? I'll say it as it is - I don't like him.

I was under the impression that you two were hired to bridge the gap between City and the likes of Real Madrid and Barcelona. And yet over 6 months later, those two clubs still seem to be a bigger draw to players. Do you not consider yourself to have failed? Will you be resigning? I won't hold my breath. If I had such a catalogue of failure at the bank I work in, I'd have been out on my ear ages ago.

So this is a plea from all City fans, on whose behalf I speak. Get your act together, make us proud, and restores some superbia (pride) in our proelio (battle) to be the bestest team in the world. It's the least we deserve.

The Various Stages of a Football Outrage

A footballer does a BAD THING. To make matters worse, the referee doesn't punish him at the time of the incident.

Twitter goes into meltdown.

The offender's manager comments that he isn't that sort of player.

High profile player? The Sky Sports Trial begins.

This can last weeks, more than a real-life murder trial. It begins with a 24/7 looping replay of said incident. This incident will be slowed down to virtually a standstill and replayed from numerous angles.

An ex-player who can just about (on a good day) string a sentence together will be wheeled into the studio to give his views, which will include being horrified, may well contain a hint of xenophobia (if the offending player is from foreign parts), and will probably hark back to the good old days.

Ollie Holt will bemoan the lack of black managers in the game.

An ex-referee may also be called upon to give his expert opinion.

These opinions will then appear as news articles on Sky's (and many others') websites.

If this is a very high-profile club, there may be the need to interview a police commissioner.

"If he'd done that in the street, he'd be arrested," the commissioner will state with a straight face.

(Let's face it, we all know someone who has served " time" after going in knee-high on someone with a slide-tackle outside Greenhalgh's.)

Finally, Sky may merge in some "vox-pops" with members of the public, though only those that are disgusted and wish to repeat the line about him being-arrested-if-he-did-that-in-the-street.

Articles will now appear in newspapers. At least one football journalist will unfavourably compare football to rugby, or if the incident occurs during a certain year, the Olympics. Ollie Holt will bemoan the lack of black managers in the game.

Fans of the club of the offending player will point out that other players have done worse things before.

Fans of the club of the offending player will point out that the recipient of the tackle/punch/stream of saliva "made a meal out of it". Mental notes will be made to boo the fouled player vociferously the next eighteen times the two clubs meet.

Reports emerge that the police are investigating the incident after a member of the public made an official complaint.

The FA announce that there will be no further action against the player as the referee dealt with it at the time.

Twitter goes into meltdown again. It crashes for three hours, meaning posting a tweet takes a whole morning.

Two hundred and seventy articles are published slamming the FA. Various journalists comment on how they have now lost all credibility. Ollie Holt will bemoan the lack of black managers in the game.

Another footballer does a BAD THING…………

Across the city, it was a difficult time at Old Trafford, though few realised just how bad, as Alex Ferguson finally retired. There was one bright spot. United, who of course give youth a greater chance than any other club in the whole wide world, had unearthed a gem. Adnan Januzaj, origin unknown, looks a great prospect, but the media fawning over him was ridiculous, though expected. I wrote this parody piece that reads almost identically to one that appeared in the Daily Telegraph soon after his debut.

Adnan Januzaj – Believe The Hype

It was the final game of the 2012/13 season. It was the end of the Alex Ferguson era, an era that finished predictably with silverware, glory and with the rest trailing in their wake. As the West Brom game came to an end, a grey cloud moved ominously over the Hawthorns and a single drop of rain fell upon the turf. We could be forgiven for believing that Matt Busby had shed a solitary tear as he watched from above, content that the legacy of Manchester United had lived on.

Sitting on the bench, next to the imperious Ryan Giggs and the legendary Paul Scholes, two players who seem to have defeated time itself, sat a young man with a young face, who did not look out of place amongst his peers. Soon the world will hear a lot more about Adnan Januzaj.

On United's popular message boards, there has been an orgasmic explosion of moist anticipation at the latest prodigy to roll off United's over-worked conveyor belt. United have carefully nurtured Januzaj since kindly taking him off Anderlecht's hands two years ago. Janujaz is special. With feet so quick he can create a sonic boom, he will mesmerize opposing players, twist their blood and leave them forlorn on the floor for decades to come. He is the link between past and present, he is United's north, their south, their east their west. He is their working week and perhaps may be their Super Sunday best.

Over at the Etihad, where oil money rules and excessive splurges on fashionable players is the norm, Manchester City's own prodigal son, Denis Suarez, a man with Archimedial levels of precision and a Socratereal reading of the game, will be quietly shuffled off to Barcelona having been blocked from the first team by Mancini's under-achievers. No one will blink an eyelid in Abu Dhabi, where PR and short-term gains are the priority. They know nothing of the prodigious talents of a young David Brightwell.

Across the borough, as David Moyes settled into his new role, sat behind his mahogany desk, surveying his new empire built on toil, sweat and dreams set amongst the stars, he will have felt a quiet satisfaction that his fruitless pursuit of players was done with the knowledge that the answer to his problems was already at the club. This may explain why United walked away from targets with a dignified silence. The future of the club is in safe hands. With Sir Alex Ferguson's guiding hand planted gently on his shoulder, metaphorically and perhaps literally, Moyes knows that he has what he needs already. And United, unlike others, know when to walk away, head held high, dignity intact.

United are not an ordinary club of course. Are they even a club at all? No, more of a concept, a state of mind, a freedom of expression woven into every seat and blade of grass in England's premier club ground. Edvard Munch, Francis Gruber and Ramón Castellano de Torres would be at home on the banks of the Bridgewater Canal.

And as the ground-staff finished off clearing the pitch after Rio Ferdinand's emotive testimonial on Friday night, a solitary dove swept down from the heavens and settled near one of the goals. A cynic might suggest that it was looking for food. The more romantic of us, those that have experienced this club's rich history woven onto the tapestry that is our heart or something, might speculate that it had sensed something special on that hallowed turf. Tales of glory, of fulfilled dreams, the roar of the Stretford end as they swayed as one, roaring on another young hero. Now it is Adnan Januzaj's turn. He steps into shoes that have ruled the world, organically. And like those before him, he is ready, as Moyes' Marvels begin a new chapter in a glorious history.

"As soon as Manchester United showed an interest, I knew where my destiny lay," said Adnan yesterday. "You do not say no to such an opportunity."
The man spookily born precisely 1000 days after United's first trophy win under Alex Ferguson says all the right things off the pitch, but is letting his feet do the talking on it. The future, as always, is bright.

Adnan Januzaj was speaking as a Nike ambassador, part of a Mahee promotional day.
Mahee - proud to be Manchester United's official noodle partner in Asia and Oceania.

Mid-August brings not only an exciting new season, but also the giddiness of the Champions League draw. This draw of course goes on for several days and tests the most patient of fans, but there was another angle that intrigued me, namely the ridiculous rules that UEFA enforced on the draw that made the thing almost pre-determined. This was my review of the draw.

The Sham of the Champions League Draw (Parody)

In an EXCLUSIVE, I reveal how the Champions League draw, held over 7 days in Monaco was nothing more than a farce, a pre-ordained process that allowed nothing to chance in its eventual outcome. The headlines may have been made by BALLGATE, which left Billy McNeill in tears, Michael Owen with a dislocated shoulder and ended with Luis Figo brawling with Michel Platini in a hotel lobby at 4am (due to the new Adidas Excelsior balls, which the manufacturers claim are more aerodynamic than any previous cup draw balls), but it was in the draw itself where the real scandal lay.

The draw has a number of caveats and rules that shapes who plays who. There are two coloured halves of the draw, and rules on teams from the same country, plus 74 other directives not known to the general public – until now.

Arsenal came out of the Pot Bowls first, and were drawn into Group F. So far so good. Then Chelsea came out of the pot and were placed into Pot C. The rest of the top seeds were drawn, and everything was fine. The draw for the second seeds began. Marseille were drawn into Group F, but this caused a problem, as their third kit clashes with Arsenal's European 2nd away kit, so they had to be moved to pot D. AC Milan were drawn into Group H, then CSKA Moscow were drawn into Group D, but Marseille were already there, so they had to be moved into pot F. PSG went into Pot C, and the other second seeds were drawn without any problems, apart from when a drop of gel fell into Luis Figo's eye and, temporarily blinded, he went down clutching his knee. The 10-minute delay was filled with a montage of previous draw highlights, including the infamous 1997 draw which descended into farce when one of the delegates did not have a pen and paper to write the draw down on.

The draw for the third set of seeds though was a scandal. Manchester City and Manchester United were both drawn in the blue half of the draw, which isn't allowed as two teams from the same city cannot play at home on the same night. So United were moved to Group B due to their superior coefficient. Unfortunately this meant City had to move from Group C as they can't be in a pot that is only 1 letter away from a team from the same city as this would compromise TV deals. So City were moved to Group D. Next out of the pot were Basel. They were immediately excluded from Pots A,B,D & E as past Champions League winners cannot be drawn in the group stage against a team that sounds like a herb. This left only Pots C ,G and H, as they couldn't go into G either due to possible clashes with Viktoria Plzen, and UEFA rules stress that any team named after a girl must not be paired either with a herb, a Portuguese team (the Portuguese secretly lobbied for this rule prior to the 2006/7 draw, having previously gone out of Europe to the little known Romanian club Lily Plovdiv), or a team that won the European Cup in the 1960's. As Basel had to be in the blue half of the draw due to a TV deal with a Czech TV station specifying they would play on a separate night as Viktoria Plzen (the station pandering to the huge Swiss population in the Prague ghettos), Basel were drawn into Group H, but had to be moved to C anyway because AC Milan were already in H and Basel can't be drawn against a team from Milan in a group stage due to sub clause c(ii), section 14 in the UEFA Champions League draw guideline document.

Then it emerged that Arsenal couldn't play in Group F as this would mean playing a home game that clashed with the National Cheese Festival at Olympia, whilst PSG requested no games on Tuesdays as they didn't want supporters to miss out on a re-run on Canal+ of the 3rd season of Luther (with subtitles). Then someone pointed out that Chelsea couldn't be drawn in the same half of the draw as Arsenal so were placed in Pot A, but this left to a fixture clash with United, so this was fixed by Borussia Dortmund swapping Groups with Bayern Munich, Shakhtar Donetsk outbid every club for the right to be drawn in Pot E, and CSKA Moscow had to have their home games moved to pre-December due to weather concerns. This meant Manchester City would be playing at home to CSKA on the same night as both Sarah Millican and Sean Lock were in town, so the kick-off had to be put back to midday, which thankfully suited the Asian markets. City agreed to play that game in their new third kit in return for a promise not to draw Barcelona at any point in the competition.

As Real Madrid's pitch was to be used for a Nickelback concert on 26th November they had to be away that night, meaning a further swap of fixtures. This swap though would leave Manchester United & City once more playing on the same night, so for no reason Real Sociedad were moved to Group F to avoid fixture clashes. This left Chelsea in limbo so they were moved to Group G, City were temporarily placed in two groups, bringing a $15,000 fine from UEFA, before switching back to Group C. Austria Vienna played their joker card to be moved from Group H, and were moved to G, leaving Celtic in the Group of Death (H), causing Neil Lennon to go on a 2-hour rampage around Parkhead (leading to the despatch of a police helicopter).

Anderlecht were placed into Pot C so that their fixtures did not clash with Yom Kippur. Ajax requested special dispensation for Match Day 3 as their players fasted every 4th Tuesday, and Zenit St Petersburg delegates stormed out of the conference hall complaining about the standard of borsch.

With one final demand from the Manchester United delegation, who requested no home matches on Matchdays 2 & 4, as "the trams will probably break down those days", the draw was finally completed shortly after midnight. But the shocking details of that draw show that it is little more than an exercise in maintaining the status quo and assuring that the "big boys" get exactly what they want. For the cheeky upstarts like Manchester City, there was the desire to put them in their place once more. Only a sold-out Sean Lock tour and a kit clash with Borussia Dortmund's home kit and City's 1999 play-off final kit prevented them from being in an even harder group.

The A to Z of City Legends

Agueroooooooooooo. A good place to start, and no further explanation is required really. What's more, he is always smiling, which is both endearing and also annoying as it's a constant reminder of just how much better his life is than mine (and yours). (Apologies Malcolm Allison. It's a stupid way to devise a list)

Bell, Colin. Nijinsky. Not because he is hung like a grand-national winner (thanks for that Lord Flashard, Edmund Blackadder's wife-stealer), but because of his tremendous stamina, and the king because of his sublime, supreme elegance on a football pitch. To many, he will always be City's greatest player, and the fact that he alone has a stand at the Etihad named in his honour says it all. Not surprising that a nasty tackle from a United player ended his career.

Coton, Tony. Really?! Yes, really, he was a bloody good keeper, and he had a bushy moustache. Then he spoiled it all by going to United. But I'm keeping him in because I'm not quite convinced enough by Gerry Creaney's credentials.
(Oh ok, it should be Joe Corrigan really)

Dickov, Paul. Scored an important goal once. Said goal resulted in me catapulting four rows down Wembley's west stand and picking up significant bruising, not that I cared. The rest, as they say, is history.

Eric Brook. No, me neither. City's all-time record goal-scorer from the inside-left position. From 1928-1939 he made 450 appearances for City, scoring 158 goals. He also scored 10 goals in 18 appearances for England. Brook scored a 'wonder goal' in front of a record crowd of 84,569 against Stoke City in the sixth round of the FA Cup. According to Gary James, 'many fans from the 1930s claimed it was the greatest City goal ever scored at Maine Road'. A fractured skull from a car crash ended his career, not that a world war particularly helped either.

F

Goater, Shaun. Feed the goat and he will score. The most recognisable of chants, even if it makes no sense whatsoever. Perhaps said goat gets horny on a full stomach? Anyway, leaving aside the early scepticism from many a city fan at Goater's prowess on a football field, he soon won everyone over, and was a true goal-scorer with a winning smile and all the attributes to attain cult status. A god back in Bermuda, he even has his own day (21st June). I bet Dwight Yorke doesn't.

Horlock, Kevin. If you shower eternal gratitude on Paul Dickov, then you must acknowledge the player that made THAT moment possible, in the same way that there would have been no league title without Edin Dzeko. So all hail the All-England Aggressive Walker Champion, the Twitter United-fan-baiter and all round good guy, with a left foot so cultured team-mates were known to kiss it after he scored.

Ireland, Stephen. The man with 16 grand-parents. Oh to spend 10 minutes inside his head. Oh to have his fish tank (he can keep the pink car though). A wonderfully-talented player, but not the first of his type to never reach his full potential, his stock having fallen so far he now plays for StokeCity.

Jimmy Grimble. I'd love to honestly say that this was a wonderful film. I really would.

Kinkladze, Georgi. "Better than David Silva," said one blue on a City message board last month. He wasn't, because being a great footballer is about a lot more than skill alone, and a player superior to David Silva would not have moved on to Derby County. But let's not quibble over one of the most naturally talented players to put on a sky/laser/all the other shades of blue shirt. It's just a shame he was at the club at completely the wrong time.

Lee, Franny. His legacy may be somewhat tainted, but without his chairmanship we'd never have experienced the Shirehorses' Ballad of Franny Lee, so every cloud and that.

Maine Road. God bless its misshaped stands, outside toilets, massive floodlights, surrounding terraces, cantilever roof, Gene Kelly stand and the plastic bird hanging down from the Kippax roof. But most of all, god bless its memories.
1923-2003.
(Tough luck Andy Morrison, Billy Meredith and the colour maroon)

Negouai, Christian. A City career that summed up the club of old. Blighted by Cityitis throughout his brief stay, the man for whom Kevin Keegan predicted superstardom stumbled from disaster to disaster. Keegan said he was the most exciting player he had seen, and exciting is certainly one way of describing his time at City.
An appalling home debut capped with a goal palmed into Rotherham's net set the tone nicely. A red card at Blackburn capped off his first spell nicely (he was rather harshly sent-off, I might add), before severe injury derailed the inevitable meteoric rise, but there was still time for a quick return to action and a goal in the UEFA Cup, a missed drugs-test, a loan spell in Austria, a revelation as a reserve striker, another injury, and a further red card after 3 minutes on the pitch, before his eventual disappearance. A cult hero was born.

Oakes, Alan. City's record appearance holder, with 680 appearances between 1959 and 1976. In his time at Maine Road, Oakes became part of more trophy winning sides than any other Manchester City player in history. In 2005 he was inducted into City's Hall of Fame.

Paul Lake. Wonderfully-talented, a diamond in the rough, but cruelly blighted by injury, and woefully treated by many at the club. Thankfully he had the strength to fight back, and move on, and still love the club like we do. Also the (co-) author of the best football autobiography I have ever read.

Quinn, Niall. Oh Niall, why did you have to ruin it all by pursuing a media career and being absolutely rubbish? By virtue of his surname he was always making the list, a disastrous 10-minute substitute appearance would have sufficed, but he was a great servant to City, and had "surprisingly good feet for a big man". He played 244 games for City, scoring 77 goals. He also once said hello to me in JD Sports.

Roberto Mancini. First trophy in 35 years. First title in 44. 6-1 at Old Trafford. Boosted scarf sales. Didn't give a f**k what people thought. Nuff said.

Sheikhs. Thanks for everything. But when are you going to serve real ale inside the ground? And where's the WIFI? Oh, and.....

Terry Christian. Yes, that's right. It's people like Terry that remind me, even when times are tough, why I am glad I am a Manchester City fan. Terry Christian is a modern-day martyr. I salute you Terry (but I've had to un-follow you on Twitter). (Oh ok, not really – it's got to be Trautmann, Bert – – no further text really required. If you haven't already, do check out one of his biographies, it's one hell of a story.)

Uwe Rosler. Grandson of a Luftwaffe pilot (*Editor: Can you check this please*), 177 appearance, 64 goals. All round good guy, has made me want Brentford (and now Wigan) to do well.

Vincent Kompany. Michel Vonk cruelly overlooked, but we can't have this list without City's inspirational captain.

Wright-Phillips, Shaun. He feels like one of us. He was great, but not the greatest and he played with a smile on his face, he terrorized many a defence, scored many stunning goals and for a while was our only shining light. Times have changed since then, but I won't forget the pride of him pulling on an England shirt for the first time and scoring too.

X Erm, well, err – Xavi? Bear with me. <fires up google>. Just one minute. Almost there. Right, here we go:
Xavi helped Barcelona win the 2009 Champions League Final versus Manchester United, which ended 2–0, assisting the second goal by passing the ball to Lionel Messi after 69 minutes. Legend.

Yaya, yaya yaya, yaya yaya, yaya yaya toure. Kolo, kolo kolo, kolo kolo, kolo kolo toure. Yaya, yaya yaya, yaya yaya, yaya yaya toure. Kolo, kolo kolo, kolo kolo, kolo kolo toure.
For THAT goal alone at Newcastle, he is a legend, let alone the FA Cup winning contribution, but of course there is far more to him than that. The man dubbed a Barcelona reserve by Brian Reade ("seduced by the whores of world football"), he is now considered by many to be one of the finest midfielders in the world.

Zabaleta, Pablo. Last week's revelation that he doesn't eat fish and chips after all has severely weakened his reputation at City, but I have decided to keep him on the list. Everything you want from a player, and more.

And so to another yearly review, or what I could remember of the year anyway. This year wasn't quite as good as the previous one for City fans, to put it mildly. You can't win them all (though with our money etc).........

2013: A Review

2013 started with a hung-over nation watching the latest almost-daily football clashes through bleary, blood-shot eyes. So the same as every other year then.
Within days, Mario Balotelli was back in the news as he grappled with manager Roberto Mancini in training. It made headline news, but no one really cared any more. Wild speculation ensued that Balotelli's time at the club was over, and that Mancini was losing the plot. For once the speculation was right. Balotelli exited first to Milan and not surprisingly ended the year back on sale.

One Daily Mail commenter had strong views on the matter:

So the Arab 'benefactors' have brought shame and pity to football, an unflattering, unprofessional, nasty, pantomime, an embarrassing antics roadshow to Manchester. Whatever words we chose, it's just not right. Like all human endeavour, sport should earn its awards through striving, consistency and dedication over a period of time. Sugardaddy demands for immediate, unearned purchase of success, brings nothing but embarrassment, shame and yes pity to a small but once decent club like City.

As the nation unwittingly chomped on horsemeat the issue of ticket prices was in the news as City returned some of their allocation for the match at Arsenal. City won at the Emirates, but with United defeating Liverpool earlier in the day, retaining the Premier League title was looking less likely by the week. Vincent Kompany was once more sent off for a clean tackle, though amazingly this time the card was later rescinded.
Three days later Paul Scholes committed a far worse tackle against West Ham but there was no media outcry for the lovable, shy family-man despite his late lunge missing the ball by 5 yards and completely taking out an opposition player.

In the heart of the city Michael Johnson was photographed enjoying fried food rather too much for a supposed footballer, and it soon emerged that City had given up on the wayward star. Across town, a new star was born and of course hyped beyond all belief:

Daily Telegraph Article Header
Meet Crystal Palace striker Wilfried Zaha – as tough as Maradona and as skilful as George Best

He would soon be usurped by an even bigger talent as United's miraculous youth system churned another Busby Babe off the production line.

City continued to progress through the FA Cup once more – having defeated Watford, Pablo Zabaleta put Stoke City to the sword. Elsewhere, Eden Hazard was sent off for kicking a ball-boy in the ribs after the 17-year old had seemingly fallen asleep on top of the ball. The boy reacted much as Suarez would after being gently brushed on his thigh – i.e. as if he had just been shot at Ypres. Overnight he became a Twitter sensation because that's how the world works now until everyone moved on bored the next day when they realised 17-year-old ball-boys don't have much of interest to say (like 39-year-old bloggers in many ways).

A home draw against Liverpool pretty much extinguished City's title hopes, Aguero's magnificent equalizer soon forgotten. Worse was to follow though with a horror show at Southampton, Gareth Barry scoring the first of two emphatic City own-goals in the calendar year. In the cup however progress continued, as two championship sides from Yorkshire were easily defeated and another trip to Wembley was secured.

Thankfully the Champions League provided ample opportunity for bitter blues to have a good laugh at United's expense as they went out of the competition to Real Madrid. According to twitter it seemed the red card for Nani was one of the worst decisions ever made. Needless to say, it was nothing of the sort.
James Lawton at the Independent called it an assault on natural justice and I laughed myself to sleep.

Meanwhile, over at The Sun:
20th March 2013 – TOURE: GIVE ME A NEW CONTRACT BY SATURDAY OR I'M OFF

Two weeks later Yaya Toure signed a new 4-year contract.

City triumphed at Old Trafford, but it changed little and then the Iron Lady popped her clogs and half the country celebrated wildly, the other half, or less, mourned and got angry. This should have nothing to do with football, but inevitably there were calls, mostly from Tory donors such as Dave Whelan, for a minute's silence before Premier League matches – after all, what could possibly go wrong?

Soon a new joke was born.
A Manchester City fan walks into a bar near Wembley.
"The usual?" asks the barman.

City were back in London and progressed to another Cup Final with a 2-1 win over Chelsea. The latest hammer-blow through the collective heart of the English football fan came soon after with the announcement that the 2013 FA Cup final would kick off at 5:15pm. Guardian journalist Jacob Steinberg commented that it was hardly a surprise that some people now treat the FA Cup with indifference if the FA can't be bothered protecting it and fans.

A pitiful defeat at Spurs finally signalled the end of City's title campaign. No red Champ20ns t-shirts were being thrown in the bin this time round, as United clinched the title with time to spare.
And with the title secured, the time had finally arrived. Alex Ferguson was finally retiring, and he meant it this time. Half a city rejoiced and it helped buoy the mood further before a trip to Wembley for the FA Cup Final against Wigan. Everything was falling nicely into place.

And then of course City lost the FA Cup Final. The uncertainty over the manager's future seemed to deeply affect a team that barely turned up to contest the match. A torrential downpour on exiting the stadium just capped off the evening perfectly, and the night was spent drowning many sorrows.

And then Mancini exited stage left. Having alienated most of the people he worked with, he fell on his sword, the perfectionist at an imperfect club. The papers went to town on his autocratic reign

By the end of the year though, I had heard from too many places that the rumours had all been true.

And so finally Norwich came to town. A limp home defeat, appalling defending, strange team selections, rumours of City's captain thumping another player – normal service for City had resumed.
Throw in a public spat between Kolarov and a whole stand, Kompany with a face like thunder and a mostly-empty stadium to greet the lap of (dis)honour, and it was a fittingly miserable end to the season. And that was that. The season over with a whimper.

The summer was long as it lacked football, bar the odd post-season friendly tour to the Big Apple, an Audi Cup, pre-season friendlies and the hugely entertaining Confederations Cup. Hey, City even created a new club just for the hell of it.

The appointment of Manuel Pellegrini was a "done deal" for almost a month, with the odd story coming out of Real Madrid wanting him, Barcelona wanting him, PSG wanting him, then Porto wanting him. In the end it was said to be a small contract dispute that delayed the inevitable, but eventually the announcement of City's new manager was made, though it was not until the first days of July that Pellegrini actually got his feet behind an Etihad Stadium desk.

City fans raised £7000 to put an advert in the Gazzetta Dello Sport thanking Roberto Mancini, a nice touch, but I had better things to spend my money on, like PPI payments and salt and pepper spare ribs.

Carlos Tevez moved on, signing for Juventus, the old lady, on a 3-year deal, whilst Wayne Rooney looked on in envy. Tevez's stay at City has seemed to run parallel with his old manager Roberto Mancini. Both seemed poised to leave as soon as they arrived (if you believed the press), both were successful but flawed, their baggage enough to incur a £10,000 surcharge with Ryanair.
Isco moved on also – to Real Madrid, and an entire fan base wailed long into the night after realising a 13,000 page thread on Bluemoon had all been for nothing.

City moved quickly (for once) and tied up the majority of their summer transfer business with six weeks of the window remaining, replacing two departed strikers with two new additions, whilst also bolstering the midfield with two other signings, all done in the nick of time as Manchester's once-in-a-decade hot-spell came to an end. Suckers!
But at the end of another tedious window, another unsung hero went for pastures new, as Gareth Barry moved to Everton on loan, effectively ending his City career.

Prior to that and City put on a pre-season party, namely City Live at Manchester Central. As with anything the club does it split the fans, with many not willing to pay £25 to see the players on a stage, so they didn't pay and others did and the others went and had a good night.

Jamie Oliver introduced his pukka bespoke pies and burgers to the Etihad, which taste much like the old ones but for more money. Nice chips though.

City somehow contrived to lose at Cardiff, the home side's red home shirts sending too powerful a force for City to resist as their buffoon of an owner looked on with his pants up to his shoulders and a moustached that shouted "bow before me mere mortals". Eat your heart out Simon Cowell. Sadly poor away form was to hamper the club for the rest of the year, further defeats to Aston Villa and Sunderland still yet to be explained by the planet's brightest boffins. At home though, City were an irresistible force, swatting away mid-table teams like Norwich City, Swansea City and Manchester United.

Mick Hucknall, Terry Christian, Eamonn Holmes, James Nesbitt, Mumford and (bloody) Sons, Terry Christian again, Zoe Ball, Paddy Crerand, Lou Macari, the chosen one, Clayton Blackmore, Terry Christian again, Mark Ogden, Usain Bolt, Gary Neville, Howard Webb, some bloke who used to present Play School, Terry Christian again. Your boys took one hell of a beating.

There was proof that Stevan Jovetic exists as City put five past Wigan in the Capital One Cup. Then Bayern Munich came to town and put City to the sword. It would seem revenge would be needed once more.

Elsewhere and Alex Ferguson released his latest instalment of his memoirs, a predictably myopic view of events that conveniently whitewashed the awkward moments in his career, omitting the Glazers' influence on the club, his fall out with the previous owners that led to the American takeover or his son's role as an agent. He even forgot to mention his speeding ticket and bowel evacuation caused by a dicky stomach. If you've ever had a session on Holts bitter, you'll understand his predicament.
The best bits were left for City though, which was nice. Of the 6-1 Old Trafford massacre, he commented:
"There was never a point where City looked superior to us."
"We battered them."

No one really cared about the past though, because it was all about the future. A new star had been born, a mix of Beckenbauer, Maradona, Duncan Edwards (obv) and Eusebio. Adnan Januzaj had arrived. And that wasn't the only good news across town. Unilever became United's 'personal care and laundry provider in SE Asia' and Mamee their official noodle partner in Oceania and beyond. Manda Fermentation Company become the club's 'Official Nutritional Supplements Partner'. On the downside, United launched an investigation into a "completely inappropriate" Nazi Swastika-style logo on their club email. People are so picky sometimes.

Harry Redknapp too released an autobiography, which needless to say was largely fabricated (allegedly). Apparently Spurs only had two points from eight games when he took over (news to me). Next you'll be telling me Dave Whelan once broke his leg in a cup final.

New figures released showed Sam Allardyce to be the 13th highest-paid manager in the world. Harry Redknapp is 26th (Pellegrini 10th).
The biggest scandal was yet to come though when two players were seen exchanging shirts at half-time. Oh, the humanity, and so soon after Flamini wore a long-sleeved shirt, urinating on over a century of Arsenal's history in the process.

City's away form slowly improved, and peaked as the team triumphed in Munich, finishing their Champions League campaign with three away victories. Sadly Manuel Pellegrini's rudimentary grasp of mathematics saw City fail to go for the jugular, namely a 4th goal that would have seen them top the group and as a result a tasty double-header against Barcelona awaits in late winter. West Ham stand between City and another trip to Wembley in the Capital One Cup and Blackburn host 7,000 inebriated City fans in the New Year. A hectic month awaits after a year that has never been dull as City continue to write the headlines for Fleet Street's finest and worst.

And so a storm-ravaged country crept towards the end of the year, and with the Premier League title race closer than it has been for many a year, here's to another exciting year of football, England sweeping all before them in Brazil and on a more realistic note for David Moyes not to be sacked, as he is doing a great job.

Tweets of The Year

Eamonn Holmes, after the appointment of David Moyes – *THE LEGACY LIVES*

@footyaccums – *City buying Negredo for £24m is such a bad piece of business. So many better strikers out there for that price.*

Bob Cass – *Jones is again the play-anywhere diamond for England. When he finally gets a crack at central defence, he'll be one of the world's best.*

Rob Beasley – *Klopp n Lewandowski to Chelsea. Jose n CR7 to Utd*

Peter Spencer, MEN: *"You won't get me saying jones is the new duncan edwards - yet"*

Jones the new robbo?

Said Baines for utd 2 years ago...great to be right for once

Its Ronnie utd really want believe it

Fgkljhgfoigjhofgiigfo

(Pete hasn't quite mastered tweeting just yet, bless).

Stewart Gardner - *Makes a nice change for Kompany and Aguero to appear in front of a full house...*

Piers Moron - *And you know what @SamNasri19 ? Arteta's a better No8 for us than you ever were. #Arsenal*

Neil Ashton: *City 4 United 1. Could be the day English football died after City start with ten overseas outfield players.*

Joey Barton – *I'll just re-iterate for a lot of the buffoons tweeting me. I WILL NOT BE PLAYING IN THE CHAMPIONSHIP NEXT SEASON. Hope that clears that up!*

Favourite Quote

"A Marseille player, whose name I don't remember, speaks badly of Neymar, Brazilian football, Beckham and Ibra. As no one talks about him, maybe he thinks he'll drool over the big players so that we know he exists. It makes me want to win even more, to shut this Englishman up. What does he know about Brazilian football? I can't remember playing against him for the national team." **– Thiago Silva on Joey Barton**

Other stuff

What Suarez said, what Terry said, was for private consumption, no matter how unpalatable. It was abuse, pure and simple. Horrid, racist abuse, **but ultimately meaningless. –** Martin Samuel column.

The index in Sven Goran Eriksson's autobiography:
Relationships with women 255, 267-8, 283-4.
See also Alam, Faria; Caprioglio, Deborah; Dell'Olio, Nancy; Jonsson, Ulrika; Mancinelli, Graziella; Pettersson, Ann-Christine 'Anki'; Yaniseth

2013/14 Predictions – Louise Taylor

League Winners

Tottenham. Europa League involvement and the potential loss of Gareth Bale are worries but Roberto Soldado and Paulinho look excellent signings and AVB is a class coach.

Player of The Season

Hatem Ben Arfa. Providing he stays fit, Ben Arfa belongs on a different planet to most mortals. Capable of eclipsing Rooney, Bale and even Suárez.

Signing Of The Summer

Paulinho. A sort of Brazilian Frank Lampard, his ability to score freely from midfield promises to transform Spurs.

Manager To Watch

Paolo Di Canio. The self-styled "revolutionary" is clever enough to confound his many critics and lead a reborn Sunderland into the top 10.

Football in 2014: Some Predictions

A stormy New Year saw an endless run of football continue unabated. Adnan Januzaj was booked for diving, a decision that David Moyes called scandalous. United were linked with Wesley Sneijder, obviously. They were also linked with various other players they had no intention of signing. The United-fed media PR campaign commenced, as £100m war-chests were announced, which soon rose to £150m then £200m. Unfortunately David Moyes and the Equalizer could still not find any value in the market.

Manchester City won 7-1 at Newcastle, but Alan Hansen was not happy with City's defending for the Newcastle goal. In the Match of the Day studio he spent 15 minutes pulling apart the positioning of Michael Demichelis, demonstrating his weaknesses with a life-size mock-up of the St. James Park penalty area and various inflatable dolls.
Words and phrases used included "sloppy","poor,poor defending", "got to do better than that", "amateur" and "capitulation". Alan Shearer called the score-line flattering.

Arsene Wenger took a bold and brave plunge into the market and purchased a new coat, which very much resembled his old one.
He said: "I have never been afraid to spend when necessary. The old coat had developed a small tear in the hood."
Manchester United target Koke signed a new deal with Atletico Madrid. The Telegraph reported that United never submitted a bid as David Moyes and his coaching staff were not convinced about his upper body strength.

There were three weeks of riots in north London after Theo Walcott blew a kiss to Spurs fans when being substituted. Adnan Januzaj was booked for diving, a decision that an exasperated David Moyes called scandalous.

Joe Kinnear announces on a radio interview that Newcastle are looking to sign Luke Remmie and Patrick Ever and sell Joan Cabby and Shola Amoeba.

Manchester United signed a sponsorship deal with Autoglass.
"Love United, hate glaziers? Then come to Autoglass for all your cracked-screen needs."
(T & Cs apply, policies not covered by acts of god or run-ins with the Men In Black)

And then the news everyone dreaded. The news that blew a hole through England's excellent World Cup chances. Wayne Rooney broke his metatarsal once more chasing after a referee in a league match in late March. The diagnosis was bleak. Two months out.

"ROO META RIO KO," screamed The Sun.
"Wazza Disazza for Roy's Lions," said The Mirror.
"England To Suffer Wettest Summer in 50 Years," said the Express.

Vigils were held outside Rooney's house. A gaggle of reporters stood forlornly outside a hospital wall waiting for some news. Any news. Viewers were treated to aerial shots of the hospital roof. A nation prayed.

Manchester United signed a sponsorship deal with Durex, who became the club's exclusive pregnancy-avoiding partners in South Asia, Oceania and Peru.

After Newcastle lost to Sunderland a Newcastle fan was arrested at Knowsley Safari Park for punching an ostrich.

Manuel Pellegrini mistakenly celebrated a title win for Manchester City after thinking it was four points for a league win. In the end the title went to Chelsea after Jose Mourinho wore down his competitors with his mind-games, a win he celebrated, due to a touchline ban, from inside a laundry basket.

Manchester United and Liverpool went head-to-head for fourth place, the battle of the two teams with the most history, apart from all those teams formed before them. In the end United just prevailed, thanks to a trio of Ashley Young-won penalties in the final match against Southampton. Adnan Januzaj was booked for diving, a decision that a haggard-looking David Moyes called scandalous.

Alex Ferguson continued to look on from the stands, fiddling with his coat as the empire burned.

Bayern Munich won the Champions League once more to complete a quadruple, and celebrated by organically buying Borussia Dortmund's best two remaining players.

RACE FOR RIO

Wayne Rooney's race for fitness went to the wire. Roy Hodgson named him in his squad, but he wouldn't be fit for the first two group games.
Phil Jones' face went a colour previously unknown to man as he lolloped around the Amazon basin, and England's post-golden generation exited the competition with a whimper after a penalty shoot-out loss to Switzerland, who wrongly had two goals disallowed during normal time. Lee Cattermole was sent off after 17 minutes. Greg Dyke was seen mimicking a cut-throat gesture in the direction of Roy Hodgson close to the players' tunnel.
The following day the Sun replaced Hodgson's head with an aubergine. Ashley Cole later starred in a Pizza Hut advert, Phil Jones in a Dulux one.

The World Cup was eventually won by Argentina in dramatic circumstances as Sergio Aguero fired in a last-minute winner against hosts Brazil in what he later called "the second-best moment of his career". The final score was 4-3, though Alan Green called the match "poor" and the stadium "a disgrace and lacking atmosphere".

Off the pitch and an ITV panel of experts consisting of Alan Shearer, Michael Owen and Mark Lawrenson creates the biggest electricity surge in British history, leaving large swathes of the country without power for days.

Roy Hodgson resigned and the nation as one turned to Harry Redknapp, freshly acquitted after a 3-week trial where he was accused of using his deceased dog

Rosie to claim widow's benefit. Redknapp claimed he couldn't read or write still so it couldn't have been him and anyway he leaves that sort of thing to the chairman. Redknapp offered to take the England job for free but the FA insisted on paying him a working wage. QPR reluctantly let him go after a plucky 7th place finish the previous seasons.

Pjanic On The Streets Of London

Headline writers whooped with glee as Miralem Pjanic signed for Spurs.
Manchester United target Ross Barkley signed a new deal with Everton. The Daily Mail reported that United never submitted a bid as David Moyes and his coaching staff were not convinced about his work-rate.
The new TV deal for Premier League clubs sees a glut of spending, even from traditionally smaller clubs. Diego Costa went to Fulham for an undisclosed fee, Thiago Silva made a shock move to Norwich City and Pedro was taken on loan by Crystal Palace.
A hectic transfer deadline day saw Peter Odemwingie ram-raiding the gates outside Fulham's ground and Harry Redknapp's failed attempt to sign Iniesta for England. Wesley Sneijder was linked with a move to Manchester United. Wayne Rooney handed in a transfer request before signing a lucrative new contract.

A new season brought new hope for all, hope that most had cruelly crushed within a fortnight.
Paul Scholes came out of re-retirement. "It's like a new signing for us," said David Moyes.
Sam Allardyce admitted that he ran the parody Twitter account in his name and that all the stories posted were true. This was not enough to save him from the sack from relegated West Ham who moved quickly and hired Glenn Hoddle, who was forced to resign after only 2 months after attributing a Carlton Cole miss as punishment for him being a brothel-owner in a previous life.
Adnan Januzaj was booked for diving, a decision that a balding, red-eyed David Moyes called scandalous

Manchester United target Juan Mata signed a new deal with Chelsea. The Guardian reported that United never submitted a bid as David Moyes and his coaching staff were not convinced about his defensive work.

Mario Balotelli returned to England as Chelsea took him on loan, but he was soon in trouble again when a game of "fire-darts" went horribly wrong at Chelsea's training ground, resulting in 3rd degree burns for two youth players.
Luis Suarez was sent off after pouring a BBQ glaze over John Terry's (left) arm and lunging in at him prior to a corner at a league match at Stamford Bridge. A subsequent 6-match ban resulted in Liverpool players wearing T-shirts in support. Adnan Januzaj was booked for diving, a decision that a wheezing David Moyes called scandalous.

The Dark Knight Rises

Adnan Januzaj was booked for diving, a decision that a sobbing David Moyes called scandalous.

Mark Clattenburg was dropped from his role at Total Hair Loss Solutions after he was seen wrestling with a Southampton player in the tunnel as the St. Mary's Stadium.

Over at the Daily Mail, Neil Ashton pens an article entitled *"The Day Football Died? Manchester City field eleven players wearing colourful boots."*

To protest against a refereeing decision in a game against West Brom, Jose Mourinho vows not to shave for 4 months. He was true to his word.

Adnan Januzaj was booked for diving. David Moyes was not available for comment.

Joe Kinnear reminisced on a radio interview about his honour at winning Time Magazine's Person of the Year. Three times.

Joey Barton called Neymar "a poncey pub-league player" on Twitter.

The traditional big teams were fighting it out for the title as Christmas approached. Promoted QPR were bottom under Harry Redknapp, who admitted his squad was down to the bare bones, adding that no manager could keep his team up.

The Qatar World Cup was finally abandoned due to concerns about the temperature in mid-summer. Sepp Blatter announced it would now be held in Canada, in the winter.

Adnan Januzaj was booked for diving, a decision that Manchester United manager Alex Ferguson called scandalous.

What I Miss About Manchester City

I miss looking up the league table with false hope or down it with trepidation. I miss reading about fights on the training ground. I miss sitting in a stand without a roof. I miss press reports about rifts in the dressing rooms and a lack of team morale. I miss the paparazzi sitting in trees at our training ground.

I miss my club spunking £3-£5m on a lower-league journeyman because he once scored against us. I miss the dead bird hanging from the Kippax roof to scare away the pigeons. I miss the abandoned games because of a waterlogged pitch.

I miss the outside toilets behind the Kippax stand. I miss the Football Pink at 6pm sharp. I miss the club paying four managers at the same time. I miss caretaker managers. I miss managers with moustaches and flat caps. I miss not seeing a goal for three months. I miss Joey Barton being our great hope. I miss the pride of a City player representing England, if only briefly and disastrously.

I miss a certain chairman's toupee. I miss queuing at the ground for five hours for a Wembley ticket. I miss play-offs. I miss terraces. I miss us playing in laser blue. I miss Buster Phillips, Ged Brannan and Kare Ingrebritsen. I miss relegation fights. I miss not winning away for a whole season. I miss our massive floodlights. I miss David Pleat skipping across the pitch. I miss paying on the gate. I miss guessing which match number the home fixture was that week.

I miss our nearest rivals hoovering up trophy after trophy. I miss us being everyone's 2nd team. I miss the frisson of excitement at the possibility of a City player being nominated (but never winning) the goal of the month competition. I miss enviously watching other fans travel to Wembley. I miss the rumours about debt and administration. I miss having to sell our one decent player to balance the books.

I miss surfing Ceefax for the latest football news. I miss playing at the Theatre of Base Comedy. I miss Eddie Large sitting on the bench. I miss him giving half-time team talks. I miss Curly Watts. I miss misshaped stands. I miss slagging off our right-back. I miss obstructed views. I miss City's season ending in January. I miss the pride at making a quarter-final. I miss the false hope of thinking that finally this might be "our year".

I miss being last on Match of the Day. Or not being on it at all. I miss barely appearing in Sky's Premier League Years, except when losing crucial matches. I miss teams beating us without having a shot on target. I miss that banner at Old Trafford.

But the truth is that apart from the Football Pink and terraces, I miss none of it. Smiley face.

But here is what I ACTUALLY miss.

I miss the walk through rows of terraces towards Maine Road. I miss it more for the night games, as I miss the lights rising up from behind the houses.

I miss standing. I miss paying on the gate.

I miss the cantilever roof on the main stand. I miss having a main stand. I miss laughing at the people in the Gene Kelly stand when the Manchester weather did what it does best.

I miss keeping the same kit for two years. I miss the Kappa kit. I miss wearing my City kit to watch the FA Cup final because it was a big occasion and kids can do stuff like that.

I miss having a season ticket book.

I miss City players with bushy moustaches (bearded Spaniards don't count).

I miss "it's a goal!" on Piccadilly 261. I miss "oh no!" less, unless it was United, which it usually wasn't.

I miss phoning premium rate numbers to get transfer gossip then denying everything when the bill came. I miss getting news off Ceefax. I don't miss missing the page and having to wait for it to cycle round.

I miss Niall Quinn's disco pants. I miss inflatable bananas.

I miss football not being about money. I miss a world that didn't need 24-hour football news.

I miss waiting for the Football Pink to be issued. I miss the match reports sometimes cutting off the last five minutes of the match.

I miss a simple offside rule.

I miss the chippy near Maine Road. I miss chips wrapped in newspaper or in a cone. I miss that last chip.

I miss the friends I made who sat around me in the Kippax. I miss standing in the same area when I was too small to see anything. I miss that first walk down the terrace steps.

I miss good commentators on the telly. I miss John Motson being on top of his game. I miss Grandstand and Saint & Greavsie.

I miss Ali Bernarbia and Andy Morrison and Shaun Goater.

I miss local pre-season friendlies. I miss my maroon socks.

I miss going to away games when the result didn't really matter.

I miss the evening after we won the league, I miss losing a football match not feeling like the end of days.

I miss wanting City players to always represent their country.

I miss collecting football stickers, less so having seven Peter Beardsleys.

I miss being able to fit into my old football tops. I miss teams tossing a coin to decide which way to kick first half (if this ever happened).

I miss tackling. I miss not having to play United every season.

I miss our massive floodlights. I miss decent pubs near the ground.

I miss Subbuteo and my Wembley board game. I miss when scarves always showed just one team and I miss men at games listening to the wireless.

I rarely look back, but I miss it all. I lied about the bananas.

The Bumper Bundle of City Slurs: The Journalist Files (Part 2)

In **Part two of City Slurs: The Journalist Files**, it's time to look at more recent years. City had re-educated many a journalist over the first couple of years of the Mansour reign, but there were still plenty of dissenters.As before, the choice cuts are in bold.

A good source was always the Sunday Supplement, a relaxed forum for croissant-eating ill-informed opinion and general prejudice. One episode in particular stands out:
In it, moral arbiters and Chelsea supporters Rob "Jose's my bessie mate" Beasley and Paul "Dracula" Smith went to town on classless City.
Smith: "£220 grand a week for Yaya Toure? . **Someone must be out of their mind there**. The thing is about Manchester City is…that whole structure there is an absolute load of nonsense."
Beasley: "They've got so much money, but **morally they are bankrupt**," said the Chelsea supporter.
Chelsea supporter Smith: "They've got a manager who is clearly arrogant in his ways..it's a typical example of a club who think they can go and buy success. You wouldn't have Mourinho, a good manager, doing this, buying left, right and centre," added the Chelsea supporter.
"I don't think they'll win anything under Mancini," added the Chelsea supporter Smith.
Chelsea supporter Beasley then added: "They're the richest club in the world, but for me they are morally bankrupt. **Any man who brings in the new manager, and sits him in the stand, while they've still got a manager, and any manager who agrees to that, to sit in the stands while they've still got a manager, knowing he's going to be unveiled after the match, it's just moral bankruptcy."**
"And I hope City pay the price," said the Chelsea supporter, "I've used this word two or three times – about DIGNITY," said the Chelsea supporter.
"There's no dignity there..the posters they put up..it's not dignified," added Chelsea supporter Beasley.
"They've got loads of cash, but no class, I hope it all implodes." added Chelsea-supporting Beasley.
"Where is the structure there?" asked Smith
"There isn't," says Brian Woolnough.
Beasley added (Chelsea supporter): "Hughes knows he's up there..I mean, if that had been most people they'd have gone 'you can stick your job'..Hughes must have been absolutely fuming…"
"Football wants Fulham to win," added the Chelsea supporting Beasley.

Beasley was forced to apologise live on the show the next time he appeared for claiming that Roberto Mancini was in the stands during Mark Hughes' last game as City manager. Rob skilfully worked his apology to be under 5 seconds long.

Speaking of which, there was great criticism for City's owners at the disgraceful way they got rid of such a bright, promising young manager in Mark Hughes, who has since gone on to distinguish himself globally at various clubs. This prompted the Manchester Evening News' Pete Spencer to ask the questions none of us were asking, the best few of which are listed below:

He had nothing on Michael Calvin though, who got a bit giddy after FCUM defeated Rochdale in the FA Cup.

By Michael Calvin

His Highness, Sheikh Mansour bin Zayed bin Sultan Al Nahyan, wooed the wrong noisy neighbour.

Instead of blowing £1billion on Manchester City, he should have **donated £1million to FC United**.

He wouldn't have been able to shape a club owned by the fans, for the fans.

But, for a relative pittance, he would have become **a folk hero**.

He would have helped expose the hypocrisy of the Glazers, the unfair burden of leveraged debt.

In so doing, football's richest man would have discovered **what football is all about**. **The empowerment of a community, rather than the enrichment of opportunists**.

Faith, defiance, and the credibility of commitment.

Passion, unprocessed and deliciously unrefined.

Joy, rather than empty rhetoric, and massaged opinion.

You don't need advertising copywriters and simpering apologists to make a statement of intent.

Alienated Manchester United fans did that, when they formed a football club to give a human dimension to a protest movement.

Equally, the League pyramid cannot adequately measure the difference between City and FC United.

On paper it is seven Divisions. In essence the clubs are **separated by a chasm, which separates constructive outrage and graceless vulgarity.**

I defy anyone to watch a re-run of FC United's FA Cup win at Rochdale without a smile. Players were stripped to homemade Superman underpants by euphoric fans. They cavorted for the cameras in the dressing room, and **promised not to turn up for work on Monday.**

Their manager was wide eyed, and about to be legless. "We'll have a couple of sherberts, here and there" he promised.

I'll take Karl Marginson, before Roberto Mancini, any day of the week. **The FC United boss does need a personal website that is beyond parody.**"Roberto Mancini," it croons. "The football. The class. The champion." Strange how it didn't mention the cautious coach, the closet politician, and the **cry baby**.

Marginson used to be a milkman, reliant on boot money from the likes of Salford City and Bacup Borough.

You wouldn't catch him posing for soft-focus photos, like a 10th-rate George Clooney.

Blue Moon Rising?

I prefer **the red flares of class warriors**, which illuminated Spotland's Willbutts Lane Stand.

Money has siphoned innocence from football.

City's purchasing power is intimidating, and intoxicating to outsiders.

I came across a caricature of a marketing executive late on Friday night.

He was worried my views would compromise his commercial relationship with Eastlands.

His type – swivel-eyed networkers who couldn't spell the word integrity, let alone grasp its meaning – are everywhere.

I loathe what they represent, why they genuflect at the feet of the City hierarchy. They are prepared to overlook the positive aspects of City's problems.

Three successive defeats remind us that wealth is worthless, if used unwisely. Briefings, and counter briefings, tell a cautionary tale of **unchecked egos** and unseemly ambition.

But, with apologies to the vast majority of City fans **who will understand my disillusion**, let's light the bonfire of the vanities.

I hope Mancini crashes and burns.

I pray FC United realise their impossible dream, a third round tie at Old Trafford. And that someone, somewhere, **has the courage to inform His Highness that he needs to act. Now!**

Apropos of nothing, Mike too has his own website – check it out at michaelcalvin.com. This is ok though, as Mike has had a far more illustrious career than Roberto Mancini, as you are about to find out.

His biography reads:

Hello.

*I could go all corporate on you, and describe myself as an **award-winning sportswriter who developed a significant secondary career in performance management, strategic communications and socially-responsive sports programming.***

*But, truth be told, I'm a hack, down to my scuffed trainers. I've been lucky, **working in more than 80 countries**, watching the great, and not-so great, events of world sport.*

That's propelled me the wrong way around the planet, as a crew member on a global yacht race against prevailing winds and tides. It has pitched me into politically incorrect car rallies, around the Amazon basin and Arctic circle.

*My Mum will tell you I've **twice been named Sports Reporter of the Year, and have collected the Sportswriter and Sports Journalist of the Year award**. I've featured at the British Press awards on seven occasions, and been honoured for my coverage of sport for the disabled.*

Back to City though.

Mario Balotelli was back in the news as he grappled with manager Roberto Mancini in training. It made headline news, but no one really cared any more. Wild speculation ensued that Balotelli's time at the club was over, and that Mancini was losing the plot. For once the speculation was right. Balotelli exited first to Milan and not surprisingly ended the year back on sale.

One Daily Mail commenter had strong views on the matter:

So the Arab 'benefactors' have brought shame and pity to football, an unflattering, unprofessional, nasty, pantomime, an embarrassing antics roadshow to Manchester. Whatever words we chose, it's just not right. Like all human endeavour, sport should earn its awards through striving, consistency and dedication over a period of time. Sugardaddy demands for immediate, unearned purchase of success, brings nothing but embarrassment, shame and yes pity to a small but once decent club like City.

Last season though, the club did something unspeakably bad. Something so appalling, so pathetic, so cowardly, that they deserved all the criticism that came their way.
What did they do I hear you ask? Change the club name? Change the kit colour? Move the stadium to a new town? No, much worse than any of that. They failed to retain their Premiership crown. Here's what James Lawton thought of it all over at The Independent:

Has the Premier League title ever been surrendered so pathetically?

In the long and not always glorious history of football there may have been more **disgracefully gutless performances** than the one put in by the champions of England at Southampton on Saturday. There may also have been a more bizarre series of utterances than those which came from the mouth of the man who carried the most direct responsibility, the Manchester City manager, Roberto Mancini, but if compelling comparisons are somewhat elusive there is one thing about which we can be certain.

It is that never before can such **a miserable example of broken down professionalism, of abandoned self-respect** and a total failure to deliver a sliver of value for money (the transfer value of City's starters was approximately £206m, with substitutes James Milner, Aleksandar Kolarov and Maicon representing another £48m), have provoked less in the way of red-blooded outrage.
Another truth was much easier to grasp this last weekend. It is that City have become **a parody of a club** who might be anywhere near taking their place at the heart of European football.

Their dismissal from the Champions League was one shocking development. The tolerance of the Mario Balotelli situation was an affront to professional standards. The reinstatement of Tevez after his Munich mutiny was another compromise to **make the flesh crawl**.

When Gareth Barry scored his tragi-comic own goal at Southampton he displayed **the body language of a zombie**. It was also a reasonable way of defining the performance of most of his team-mates. It wasn't a defeat. It was a submission. It was a terrible statement about what happens when a team is **separated from any sense that it can still achieve its most basic ambitions**.
For many, it was almost entirely the fault of players grossly overpaid and seriously under-motivated.....

To be fair, he was right about that Southampton performance....

To be honest, there was something EVEN WORSE that City had done prior to that – changed the name of their new ground. As sure as night following day or a Phil Jones gurn, Ollie Holt tweeted his disgust:

There are many ways in which the current owners of Manchester City have shown class. Renaming the stadium after a sponsor isn't one of them.

I know part of the answer is FFP but if City have got so much cash, why do they have to sell a piece of their soul for stadium naming rights?

Many City fans saying they don't care about stadium renaming because new stadium never had an identity anyway. Sad comment on the game.

Is it acceptable then to change name of team too? Presumably all in favour of Etihad Stadium would be fine with Etihad City as name of team.

If you defile the stadium by prostituting its name, you destroy part of the experience.

I said this at the time: *Last night I watched a documentary on the Formula One racing driver Ayrton Senna. When Senna crashed his car and died at Imola in 1994, as the helicopter carried him away from the track, Jeremy Clarkson commented (in a rare moment of sensitivity) that it really illustrated Senna's soul departing. A nation mourned over a lost soul. It has never mourned over the name of a stadium or the wages of a football player.*

But of course we have to leave the best to last. You all know it, you've all read it, you've all sent him an abusive e-mail. So put your hands together and give a warm welcome to the one and only Brian Reade!

Take it away Brian:

(ah f**k it, the whole lot's going in bold)

How Barca reserve Yaya Toure was seduced by the whore of world football

I've read many frightening stories about footballers in the Sunday papers.

But no tale has scared me as much as the one I read in a sniffy broadsheet, last Sunday, which could have come from the business pages:

"Manchester City's new £24m signing from Barcelona, Yaya Toure, is being paid £220,000-a-week. His initial wage of £185,000 will rise to £221,000 when the 50% tax rate comes in next April. He is due to receive £4.1m a year after tax, an image rights payment of £1.65m a year and a bonus of £823,000 each time City qualify for the Champions League and £412,000 if they win the competition. He will also get bonuses if the club win the Premier League and the FA Cup. The deal including his transfer fee, wages and bonuses, totals £79.6m."

Holy. Mother. Of. Jesus. Where will that leave the price of everyone's season ticket in five years time?

Even more frightening was what that report didn't say. Toure is not actually that great. He's not a creative genius who will get backsides off seats but a defensive midfielder who stops players who can.

He wasn't even a regular at Barcelona, having lost his place to Sergi Busquets. He may not even get a game for City, who already have four highly-rated players to fill that role – Patrick Vieira, Gareth Barry, Nigel de Jong and Vincent Kompany.

And scariest of all, Toure says he only joined City because his agent "told me I had to leave Barcelona". To add insult to injury the best he could say about his move was "it's an honour to be playing with my brother Kolo," before telling Barca that he'd love to go back there if they'll have him.

If you're a City fan, I'm guessing you'll have no problems with the story. It's proof the Sheikh is more determined than ever to land you the big prizes, and after all those years in United's shade who could blame you licking your lips at the prospect.

But how do outsiders begin to describe how depressing the implications of this transfer are? I can understand luring the sought-after David Silva to Eastlands for £140,000-a-week, but giving a quarter-of-a-million quid every seven days to a defensive squad player who no other club would have touched for that kind of money and whose name won't sell shirts, is insanity on a previously unimagined scale.

See how those figures play with Carlos Tevez and Emmanuel Adebayor's agents, or the leeway it gives Fernando Torres's and Didier Drogba's advisors if they decide to listen to a City offer. What do you reckon, half-a-million-a-week minimum? See how it impacts on other clubs trying to keep pace with wage demands.

See the shaking of parents' heads when City scouts ask to let their little fella join their academy. See the disillusion on the faces of the City youngsters who won the Youth Cup two years ago.

City aren't alone. Most Premier League clubs will invest the bulk of their summer spending abroad. They're just the most extreme example of why England's national side continue to fare so badly at the big tournaments.

Our clubs sent 106 players to South Africa, and the number has already soared past 110 while the contest is still on. Serie A sent 75, La Liga 57.

Spot the link with England's woeful performances which showed the lack of quality throughout the squad. We just don't have the players. Mainly because they've had their way blocked by average, over-paid foreign mercenaries.

An objective outsider would look at the obscene amount paid to seduce Toure to England, look at the country's lamentable showing in the World Cup, and conclude we deserve our misery because we've become the whores of world football.

THE END

A Letter In Football365.com

<u>Ban This Sick Filth</u>
As Vincent Kompany wheeled away in delight after his goal against Spurs, I was reminded of the token Spanish kid I went to school with.

Jose, his name. He wasn't very good at football, but boy did he try. When we had a kick-around, he wouldn't get much of a touch. But if the keeper rolled it to his feet, he would smash it straight back in the goal and celebrate maniacally. Any kind of unsporting or unworthy goal subsequently became known as 'doing a jose'. eg. Kanu was guilty of 'doing a jose' for Arsenal against Sheff Utd that time in the cup.

Which brings me back to Kompany.

To celebrate wildly after scoring a fifth goal isn't classy at all. It was 'doing a Jose'. To do it after scoring a fifth goal against a ten-man team who had already given up any hope of scoring, from 3 yards out no less, for a billionaire club that are scoring 5 goals a game anyway, well that goes beyond 'doing a Jose'. That was simply pathetic.

The experiment is done. We've seen what would happen to a football club if you gave them unlimited resources; they score 5 goals a game. It's time for the experiment to end. It won't, and as this season wears on, the idea of this being a competitive season at the top end of the EPL will dissipate, replaced with the realisation that City have done a Sim City instead; typed in 'CASH' 50 times and built whatever they liked. To see them garner some sort of sense of achievement from it worthy of exuberant celebration is wholly depressing. I found it tasteless, classless and frankly embarrassing.

Rich Phippen

Football In The Bible

Genesis

1. In the beginning God created the Premiership and BSkyB
2. And God said, Let there be light entertainment: and there was light entertainment.
3. And God saw the light entertainment, that *it was* good: and God divided the light (Division 1) from the darkness (Divisions 2-4).
4. And God called the light THE PREMIER LEAGUE TM, and the darkness he called THE FOOTBALL LEAGUE. And the evening and the morning were the first day.
5. And God said, Let the earth bring forth grass, synthetic and real and also creosote markings.
6. And God said, Let there be floodlights in the firmament of the heaven to divide the day from the night. And let them be to give light upon the pitch: and it was so. And let not Malaysian betting syndicates remove this light; but it was not always so.
7. And God created in his own image Richard Keys and Andy Gray, though he made Richard with great hair, even on his hands.
Andy, less so.
For many years the two reigned in paradise, but wisdom was gained through disobedience at severe cost. And the lord saw that misogyny was their forbidden fruit and their downfall was a snake.
8. But before all could progress, new laws were set in place for the citizens and the devils and the pensioners and the toffees and the canaries and the Geordie tribe and the Mackems from the north and the gunners and their neighbours the spurs and more.
9. And God spoke all these words, to all, but mostly to the citizens:
10. **The Eight Commandments**
11. I am the Lord your God, who brought you out of Moss Side, out of the land of debt.
12. You shall have no other gods before me, not even David Silva.
13. You shall not murder Sloop John B songs, even if the city is yours.
14. You shall not commit adultery, unless you are a footballer or Russell Brand.
15. You shall not steal, unless it's a leverage scheme and a loose Fit & Proper test has been passed.
16. You shall not give false testimony against your neighbour by pretending they have lots of empty seats.
17. You shall not covet your neighbour's house. You shall not covet your neighbour's wife unless you are Ryan Giggs, or his male or female servant unless you are Ryan Giggs, his ox or donkey unless you are Ryan Giggs, or anything that belongs to your neighbour, unless you are Ryan Giggs.

---

1. Then hear thou in heaven, and of thy people Manchester, that thou teach them the good way wherein they should walk (with a swagger), and give rain upon thy land, which thou hast given to thy people for an inheritance and also

as a curse. And a great plague was sent down on Manchester, and it rained for 40 days and 40 nights, and then another 40 days and 40 nights, and so on and so forth for all of eternity. And yet still when the rain did relent the lord said until his people that there would be a hosepipe ban. And further plagues were sent down on the people, first swarms of glory-hunters then Monday night football then Jim White.

2. But before all this came a man with false hair to rule over the Citizens. And at first all was well and Peter (Swales) doth say this is easy, but it was not easy.
3. The people did lose heart and rebelled, refusing to enter Maine Road and crying for a new leader who would take them back to the promised land.
4. During these years of wandering in the wilderness, Swales' patience was continually tested by the murmurings, grumblings, and complaints of the people. At one point, Swales' patience reached its breaking point and he sinned against the Lord, in anger against the people, by signing Steve Daley.
5. When hence he did depart, their saviour arrived, but nothing was well still.
6. The citizens turned and took a journey into the wilderness by the way of Division 2, as the LORD spake unto them: and they compassed administration many days and many months. And the LORD spake unto them, saying, "Ye have compassed this mountain long enough: turn you northward."
7. Now rise up, and get you over the black burn. And they went over the black burn.
8. And the space in which they came from York, until they were come over the black burn was two years;

---

1. And Jesus provided many miracles, not least the return to the Premiership. And he did feed the 5000 (Fulham (H)), yet still they did run out of chicken balti pies by half-time. And Jesus said: "I have compassion for these people: they have already been with me 90 minutes and have nothing to eat, and they have been with Stuart Pearce for three years and have no goals to see."
2. And Jesus expelled the money changers from the temple, accusing them of turning the temple into a den of thieves, especially those ***** at Viagogo.
3. Thaksin was expelled into the wilderness, and he fled to the east. And all the while Sven begat Ulrika and Nancy and Faria and begat anyone who moved.
4. And the LORD said, I have surely seen the affliction of my people which were in Moss Side and now Beswick, and have heard their cry by reason of their taskmasters; for I know their sorrows;
5. And I am come down to deliver them out of the hand of the Shinawatras, and to bring them up out of that land unto a good land and a large, unto a land flowing with milk and honey; unto the place of the Mansours, and the Sheikhs, and the snazzy F1 race, and the desert, and that appalling Michael Owen helicopter video on Youtube.
6. Seriously, look it up. It's terrible.
7. If thy people go out to battle against their enemy, whithersoever thou shalt send them, and shall pray unto the LORD toward the Citeh which thou hast chosen, and toward the council house that I have built for thy name. And my followers will not care about defeat, both now and the previous week, because of inebriation. And that shall be OK.

8. And so it was noted in Leviticus (19:27): " You shall not round off the side growth of your heads nor harm the edges of your beard, and to maintain the strength of your bitterness and lies your moustache should never diminish."

---

1. Now the Philistines gathered together their armies to battle, and were gathered together at the theatre of dreams, which belongeth to Trafford, and was pitched between Manchester and Salford, in the north.
2. And there went out a champion out of the camp of the Philistines, named Alex, of Govan, whose height was six cubits and a span.
3. And he had an helmet of brass upon his head, and he was armed with a nose as red as the blood of the citizens of Bethlehem;
4. And he had by him Wayne of Rooney. And Wayne had greaves of brass upon his legs, and a target of brass between his shoulders. And this brass was as old as the hills of Mezualeb.
5. When Graham Poll and all referees heard those words of the Philistine, they were dismayed, and greatly afraid. And all the men of the FA, when they saw the man, fled from him, and were sore afraid.
6. Now Roberto was the son of that Aldo and Marianna; and he had two sons, who he placed in the reserves. And he asked what shall be done to the man that defeateth this Philistine, and doth knock him off his perch?
7. And the people answered him after this manner, saying, so shall it be done to the man that killeth him, thou shall be inducted by Garry Cook into the Manchester United hall of fame.
8. And Roberto put his hand in his bag, and took thence a billion petrodollars, and slang it, and smote the Philistine in his forehead, that the stone sunk into his forehead; and he fell upon his face to the earth.
9. So Roberto prevailed over the Philistine with silva and more, and smote the Philistine, and slew him; but there was no sword in the hand of Roberto. And during this period did all witness the Exodus.
10. And so it was only 3-1, but the crowds did depart. It was only 4-1, yet more had left. It was only 5-1, yet the empty seats were plentiful. And then it was 6-1, and the land was bare. And so it came to pass that it should have been 10. And they did thank themselves that it was not 10, and considered the good fortune of the illegitimate.
11. And it came to pass in the eighteenth year after the children of England were come out of the land of the football league, in the fourth year of Mansour's reign over the Citizens, in the month May, which is the fifth month, that Roberto finished building the house of the champions*.
12. And the City had no need of the sun, neither of the blue moon, to shine in it: for the glory of petrodollars did lighten it. And the people did say Agueroooooo. And the word of the citizens came to Roberto, saying, "Blessed are the owners, and may all their teas be chippy teas".
13. And the lord did say "Drink it in. Go forth and celebrate, for you will never see anything like this again." And they did drink it in and they continued to drink it in and some are still drinking it in.
14. But the rejoicing did wane as a great curse returned on the team. Roberto was betrayed by one of his apostles, probably the kit-man, who did travel to the Sun and tell of his master's tyrannical ways.

15. And so from a cold land came a holistic man who brought with him many goals.
16. And the knight finally departed, not only because he was of great years and his powers had waned, but also because he transgresseth by wine. But the fear of his followers, who numbered three billion and ten, were assured not to worry, as on the mountain of Sinai in the summer of the 14th year of the millennium the chalice which no one yet knew was poisoned was passed to the chosen one: David from the town of Glasgow in the north. And they did proclaim that the legacy did live on.
17. And so it came to pass. But they couldn't, because they were English, so the chosen one led his followers back into the wilderness. But behold! There was great rejoicing in the west as it came to be that they now had an official drinks partner for America and Asia.
18. And a star rose in the east, and the Lord called him Adnan. And he came from the land of Albania and the land of Belgium and the land of Kosovo and the land of the English. And he told the Lord that he did not know from whence he had come. But the Lord and all around him saw that he shone brighter than any other star, and he guided the wise men to Bethlehem and beyond, into the realm of the cusp of the Europa Cup.
19. Blessed is the war chest for it shall break open and restore the power of those in red. And the growth begins and it shall be organic, both through history and success, in the west and especially in the east, where their star shines brightest. And it will be so as is it is in their DNA. And the chosen one went forth once more and he proclaimed "we are back!"
20. But then they were defeated at home to Swansea.
21. And David did proclaim (Psalms 3:6): "I will not be afraid of many thousands of people who have set themselves against me all around." And he had by him the holy trinity, so all was well in the kingdom.
22. But more support was coming in the dark. For, lo, David did raise up the Men In Black, that bitter and hasty nation, which shall march through the breadth of the land, to possess the dwelling places that are not theirs. They are terrible and dreadful: their judgment and their dignity shall proceed of themselves.
23. They shall come all for violence: their faces shall sup up as the east wind, and they shall gather the captivity as the sand. And they shall force Rio Ferdinand to sign a new contract. But they shall not force Nemanja Vidic to stay as he leaves the chosen ones.
24. And having slain some families on Wembley Way they doth proclaim: our work is done. And it had to be so, as they did not return to the land of the twin towers for a long time.
25. **Numbers**
26. But the blue tribe had become too powerful, and the other tribes doth protest at this power, which had not been earned how they wanted it to be. And thus Michel pushed for new laws, for he was angry as he had a woman's name.
27. And one man who protested hard was Arsene Wenger, but to no avail, as in the land of the blind, the one-eyed man is king. And the weight of Arsene's coat was five thousand shekels of gold.
28. The special one did also speak, and he did speak some more, then some more and the lord said to the people "please shut up this interminable bore" but the special one was not for shutting up and he doth speak some more.
29. Jesus, crosses, blah blah.....

The A-Z of Manchester City Villains

Antic, Raddy. The first on this list and the first villain of my City-supporting life. A mere year into my bumpy journey with City and up popped Antic to condemn City to relegation and make me question if I had made the right allegiance, something I continued to question for a couple of decades. He was also responsible for David Pleat's inclusion on the list, as you will see.

Ball, Alan. Where to start? A terrible, terrible manager and it seems that telling players you once won the World Cup doesn't guarantee better performances. Who knew? A flat-cap on the touchline is not a great look either, if I'm honest. There have been so many poor managerial appointments in City's history (yes, we do have one), but Ball stands out for me.

Crerand, Paddy. There is a cast of thousands, and it would be easy to choose Eamonn Holmes, Clayton Blackmore, Lou Macari, Terry Christian, Mumford & Sons and many more, but if you were to choose one United sycophant who sees everything through red-tinted glasses, can never see any fault in their club and drones on repeatedly about history and the DNA/soul of their club, a DNA and soul that makes them more special than any other club, then this is your man, the man for all occasions.

Danny Mills. Need I say more? Well I will anyway. Happy to leech off the club for years and seems even happier to slate the club at every possible opportunity. I don't know what he has against the club and I don't care, but how the guy gets endless media jobs and onto an FA Commission is baffling.

Everton. Bogey club, c*ap restricted view, poor quality 100-year-old seats, a crowd baying for blood, with every decision that goes against them portrayed as a miscarriage of justice (see their booing of Lloris as he lay partially-unconscious on the pitch this season), and older fans will tell you what thugs a sizeable minority of them were in the 80's, and thus their hatred for them. And then there was the CHOSEN ONE's bleating over the Joleon Lescott transfer. For that alone they are on the list.
(and we lost 9-1 to them in 1906).

Ferguson, Alex. David Moyes or Alex Ferguson? A ruthless dictator who got more out of his teams than seemed feasible, the day of his retirement was a good day for City, Chelsea, Arsenal et al. In every sense of the word(s), good riddance. Check out his autobiography's mentions of City if you are ever down, it will cheer you up no end (don't buy it, obviously, just find the extracts).

Gene Kelly stand. Always amusing to watch other people dressed in cheap mackintoshes getting drenched, but come on – what a ridiculous addition to the old ground. An embarrassment, if truth be known.

Halsey, Mark. Yeah, that's right, Mark Halsey. Please spare me how he was a hero for the added time amount in the play-off final. The amount added on was correct, and merely him doing his job. Since then he seemed to go out of his way to give us nothing. Now he is whoring himself around in the pursuit of money and fame. So sod him.

Ian Rush – yes, City did what City do best by holding the ball in the corner when drawing a match they needed to win to avoid relegation, but if Liverpool had done their job and not put any effort in, as morally they should have done in a meaningless game for them (ahem), then perhaps the king of all cock-ups may never have occurred. Rush scored that day so I hold him especially responsible, in one of those irrational hatred things we all have.
(Don't we?)

Jon Macken – for scoring one outrageous goal against City on a rainy day in Preston, thus convincing our profligate manager that you were worth spending £5m on. If only it had bounced wide.

Karl-Heinz Rummenigge. Ah, the pied piper of the city-are-evil-and-are-killing-football-you-can't-disrupt-the-status-quo-we-do-things-the-right-way-and-intend-to-keep-squashing-anyone-who-gets-in-our-way-and-we'll-go-crying-to-UEFA-if-you-try-and-stop-us-or-perhaps-start-a-European-super-league brigade.
As Bayern Munich chief executive, Rummenigge likes nothing more than to bleat about City and them not meeting financial fair play rules. Thankfully his bleating seems to have been in vain whilst his own club do things the right way, organically backed by huge corporations.
The Bundesliga is all that is good in football of course and you only have to mention the league to David Conn and a change of pants is required but the likes of Ruminegge have got their way and domestic and (some European) domination has come to fruition for Bayern now. Mission accomplished.

League, Champions. Little known fact klaxon – in 1929, a young George Orwell wrote a book that was never published called 1992. In it, the anti-hero James

Grimble was conditioned to like a "brave new world" by a constant stream of propaganda that was communicated through big screens (Orwell was a visionary). This new world had shiny balls, evocative opera-lite music blasted through huge speakers 24/7, and money. Lots and lots of money. Orwell called it the Champions League, a league for champions and all their powerful friends who weren't champions but needed to stay powerful so they could keep trying to be champions along with their select group of friends. There was no resistance to this world that Orwell painted so evocatively and hauntingly. Resistance was, after all, futile. And thus City, and so many other clubs, never had a chance of success anymore without a benefactor. The beautiful game.

Michel Platini. The devil himself, in human form. The greatest trick Platini ever pulled....
I don't know if Platini is angry because he has a woman's name or he genuinely thinks Financial Fair Play is a good thing, but the fact is it addresses few of the issues in the modern game (it would not have prevented Portsmouth's woes, for example), helps maintain a status quo and was introduced only after pressure was applied from Europe's most powerful clubs, which tells you all you need to know.Any footballing great is diminished in my eyes when he becomes a politican, and that is all he is now, the rights and wrongs of the game of little concern as long as he gets along in life.

Newspapers. They all have it in for City, right? Well not really, but they sure make life difficult for City, as with any other sporting institution. From the stupid press conference questions, the agendas, the lies, the appalling agent-led transfer gossip to the pitiful opinion pieces from the likes of Harry Redknapp, Brian Reade or Ian Wright, we really would be better off without a swathe (but not all) of our football press.

Office, ticket (Maine Road). Only City could have an outside ticket office in the rainiest City in the country. The night the League Cup match v Ipswich was abandoned due to Paul Dickov almost drowning, I queued for my ticket outside a portakabin for 30 minutes, and have been dryer than I was that night when submerged in a bath. I haven't been the same since.

Pleat, David. Faster than a kerb-crawling car, David skipped across the Maine Road pitch in his loafers and one of the first memories of my City-supporting life was etched indelibly on my brain. He hugged Brian Horton on his travels that day, but Brian's a lovely bloke so I'll let him off. The previously mentioned 1-0 home defeat to Luton in 1983, condemning City to relegation from the top flight was a perfect example of what was to come. I've always held an irrational grudge against Pleat ever since, probably fortified by the opinion that he is a terrible co-commentator who can't pronounce the simplest of names.

Quinn, Niall. Another player that makes it onto the Heroes & Villains list, once I realised this is a stupid way to compile a list (wait until you see the Z entry!). Quinn gets in for his new role as simpleton-sidekick to Martin Tyler, his inane ramblings and his ability to talk drivel about City never a joy to behold. Where United have ex-pros scattered throughout the media ready to fight their corner with ludicrous levels of prejudice and bias, here is yet another ex-player all too eager to stick the boot in. I'm not saying pundits should be biased towards old teams, but everyone else's ex-players seem to be, so why not ours? How have we managed to scar every single one of them?

(don't answer that)

Revolving door. A metaphorical one. City's inability to keep one manager for any considerable period of time added to their many woes for decades and prevented any chance of stability at the club. Many managers should never have got the job in the first place of course, but the odd diamond in the faecal matter rarely stayed for too long anyway.

Swales, Peter. City's own pantomime villain. He meant well, he was after all a blue, but it's fair to say there were some terrible decisions along the way, and the Granada TV documentary that followed him around makes for some painful (and I'll admit, hilarious) viewing. The footage of John Bond's interview for the manager's job stands out. Swales' reign was never going to end well and it turned out the grass wasn't greener on the other side after all. A sad time for the club and for all concerned.

Tony Coton. Yes he is on the heroes list as well, but he left us for United, so big boos all round to him. Judas!

United, Manchester. Boo, hiss (see C,F and X for further details).

Villa, Ricky. Judging by the number of times I am subjected to it, it seems Villa scored the only great goal in the history of the FA Cup. None of us will ever be allowed to forget it. The magic of the FA Cup,eh?

Weah, George. It's stretching the definition somewhat to call Weah a villain, but he is symbolic of City's buying policy for much of the dark days of decades past. Purchasing players who used to be good was something City specialised in and Weah fit the bill perfectly, bringing with him a large pay packet (£30k a week). In the end, Weah played 3 full games for City, but at least he didn't hang around for too long and thus cost the club that much money. By purchasing players in the twilight of their career the odd gem was acquired this way (Ali Bernarbia springs to mind), but plenty of duffers passed through also. I'm looking at you Steve McManaman.

X-rated tackles. Martin Buchan, Roy Keane. There's a pattern developing here.

Yeboah, Tony. His wonder-strike (you know the one) stopped the miraculous possibility of a City player actually winning goal of the season. That's all I've got. If you think that's bad....

Z – the letter Z in the club shop printing section. Hear me out, it's the biggest villain of all. Because of City's influx of Georgian players, namely Georgi Kinkladze, Kakha Tskhadadze and Murtaz Shelia, the club shop ran out of the letter Z for the back of shirts. This caused a slump in sales of shirts in the shop as Mr Kinkladze especially was the most popular name and as the club charged by the letter, was a money-spinner for the club at a time when money was scarce (hence Joe Royle's suggestion to the board to sign the enigmatic Bulgarian playmaker Vladivar Romavaronichinov). Anyway, this slump in income was crucial in City's failure to remain competitive. A succession of poor players bought on the cheap as a result of the failure to sell shirts eventually resulted in two relegations and put the club back over a decade, brought near bankruptcy and the exit from Maine Road. Few realise it was all little Georgi Kinkladze's fault.

2013 saw the release of the greatest autobiography ever published – I am of course referring to diamond geezer Harry Redknapp. There was a small problem though – namely Harry's memory, which seemed to have failed him, as various people came out after publication to state the book was a pack of lies. So, I wrote a parody piece about Harry's selective and often convenient memory-loss.

Exclusive Extracts From Harry Redknapp's New Book

The following article is of course completely fabricated.

Dedicated to Rosie. So much more than a dog.

I live for football, always have. It has given me so much. I have no organisational skills, am rubbish with money, and am in it for the love of the game. The game has give me a bit back. Me and Sandra moved into a modest house in Sandbanks, in Dorset, and we still live there now.

But for me, it's all about finding new players, bringing on talent. In the summer of 1997 I got a call off Joe Jordan on one of those new-fangled mobile phones that were all the rage at the time – I had a Samsung Tab – anyway, Joe says he has seen a hot new kid worth looking at, from South America, went by the name of Messi. I was sceptical, but said to get him over to have a look.
He was tiny! Terrific skills, lovely lad, didn't say much, but he wasn't for me. I interviewed him in my car, and sent him on the way with a pat on the back and some words of encouragement. I hope I had helped the lad in my own way. I've heard he has done well for himself, but I don't watch much foreign football.

Then of course there's transfer deadline day. I'm not one for last-minute wheeler-dealing, but often there is the need to make the odd last-minute tweak here and there. I got wind one year whilst at the Hammers of the availability of Titi Camara. Time was of the essence, so I travelled up to Liverpool by Concorde, and by dusk a deal was secure. I stayed well away from the boardroom itself, as I leave that sort of thing to the chairman. But in the end I got the club a £10m player for £1.5m. The lad didn't suit our style, and I thought he was a terrific lad, though not the brightest, always rabbiting on about tactics and other stuff that went over my head if I'm honest, but at the time it was one hell of a coup, and it put West Ham on the map. At Portsmouth, who were in severe financial difficulties prior to my arrival, we sold Crouchy on for a nice profit. Lovely lad, but not the brightest. Terrific feet for a big lad. He had married some glamour model who I didn't much care for, and I think she had pressured him to move. It was no surprise that Portsmouth struggled after my exit – throughout my tenure there we were down to the bare bones, and in dire need of reinforcements, but there was just no value in the market. The squad I took over was rubbish – some of the lads didn't even speak English, and we had two strikers who wouldn't know a sausage roll if it hit them in the face.

At Spurs a rumour emanated that I was after Ruud Van Nistelrooy. I was soon being asked about him repeatedly in the car park at Spurs' training ground, which annoyed me, as I don't like talking about other clubs' players. Daniel Levy was desperate to do a deal, and was prepared to pay whatever it took to get the Dutchman, but I stood up for my career-long principles and insisted we couldn't go blowing silly wages on a player in the twilight of his career. Thankfully Daniel finally saw sense, though he repaid me by shamelessly sacking me soon after. Spurs only had 2 points when I took over, but football can often stab you in the back.

Of course in between my Pompey spells came a fulfilling spell at Southampton. The offer came out of the blue. Rosie was there when I got home with a wagging tail and a piece of paper in her mouth. Good old Rosie had checked my emails and got rid of the trash. Sandra read the words out to me. It seemed Southampton were interested in me as their manager. I told Sandra that I was worried how a move would be taken by the Portsmouth fans, who loved me, but I needn't have worried as they were absolutely fine with it all. It was good to go with their blessing, and it made my eventual return there all the more pleasing, and meant I could leave them for a second time (having claimed previously it would be my last job in football) with a clear conscience.

I've earned good money in my time, but I am not in it for the monetary rewards. I don't look at contracts, so I don't know why clubs keep giving me such large wages and such huge bonus payments. Sandra joked that I should give my £500,000 bonus for getting Spurs into the Champions League to charity, but there are so many good causes out there I wouldn't know where to start.

Off the pitch, I have had many good men by my side. It doesn't always work out of course. The fall out with Billy Bonds was one such occasion. There were some spurious rumours that he didn't like me hogging the pre-match limelight, but the truth is that we fell out over the most trivial of things. Billy and I were discussing the translations of Friedrich Nietzsche's seminal work Idyllen aus Messina, and a disagreement soon ensued over which was the greatest translation. When a further disagreement brewed over whether he was more greatly influenced by Heraclitus or Rousseau, there was no going back. We almost came to blows and have not spoken since.

I was the nation's choice for the next England manager, no doubt about that. I was having a leisurely breakfast at the Ocean Hotel Health Resort & Spa with Ollie Holt, and I remember quite clearly Ollie telling me that people were coming up to him in the street telling him that I had to be the next boss. I had texts too, telling me the same thing. I'm not great with technology, and can't read, but I do recall one message from Bobby Moore saying he wished me all the success in my new role, and that I deserved it. True legend was Bobby. Michael Owen text me too, saying all the lads in the England squad were desperate for me to get the job. As an aside, I tried to sign Michel whilst I was manager of Southampton, but there was no helipad at The Dell, so that scuppered the deal. I've still got his glossy brochure at home, some lovely pictures in there.

Thankfully the court case was eventually over, a simple misunderstanding blown out of all proportion, but it seems the jokers at the FA, who have never managed a club, never sold 30 players in a year, got duped by a fake jockey or appeared in a Wii advert seemed to think my reputation, previously impeccable, was now tarnished. All my trophies suddenly counted for nothing.

But I am not one to hold grudges. And I look out there now at the footballing world with pride. Gareth Bale is one of my proudest stories as a manager. I can't remember how many times coaches and assistants said to me, "Harry, you've got to play him on the right, or as a holding midfielder." So-called experts slated me for not even trying him in net, but I knew where his future lay and look at him now. I don't feel I get enough credit for that, but you win some, you lose some. Look at Andros Townsend now – I knew he was going to be a talent even when I was manager of Bournemouth, and Andros was just breaking into the Spurs' first team.

But lately it has been tough, no denying that. When I took over QPR, the team was a mess. No manager could have kept that team up, not Fergie, not Arsene, nor me. I was onto a hiding to nothing. I did my best of course, but I don't think the board understood what was needed to stay up – they bought a lot of players on healthy wages, and that's not my style at all, so it started going wrong from the very beginning. But we'll be back, as I have a good set of lads under me, and we sing from the same sheet. And apart from a £10 million house and no criminal record, who could want more than that?

These extracts were translated from the original crayon markings.

Harry Potter & The Theatre of Dreams

Little Eric Remi Jesper Busby Choccy Charlton Jones lay in bed, waiting for his father to say goodnight.

A Pete Boyle CD played softly in the background, containing all his favourite terrace anthems. His Phil Jones curtains had been drawn.

"To keep the monsters away," his dad joked as he ruffled his hair.

His bag was packed for school the next day. He had his Tom Cleverley pencil case, containing his Wayne Rooney rubber, Vidic pencil set and Van Persie fountain pen. He snuggled up under his Ryan Giggs reversible duvet. His dad set the alarm on his Alex Ferguson clock.

"What time is it daddy?"

He looked at the clock.

"Anytime you want, son."

"Can you read me a story please?"

"Of course I can son. Now, which one would you like? We've got *Harry Potter and the Theatre of Dreams*. Or maybe *The Day Eric Cantona Saved The World*. Or this one, *Remi Moses: 1997 Annual* ?

The little boy looked pensive for a moment.

"Harry Potter and The Theatre of Dreams please!"

"OK, son. Though I should point out for copyright reasons, there is no mention of Harry Potter or spells or Hogwarts or invisibility cloaks in this book. It's full of magic though…"

He cleared his throat, and began……

Once upon a time, in a stadium far, far away….

The boy Potter entered the stadium, wide-eyed in amazement at the sights before him. His dad had managed to get him a ticket! They were like gold-dust, but thankfully his father had managed to get a couple off Bobby Charlton. What a nice man.

Fans hurried to their seats. Tourists took photos. Supporters threw down their pre-match noodles, thanks to Mamee, United's official noodles partner for Asia, Oceania and the Middle East.

His dad took a long swig of the nectar-like liquid in the bottle in his hand.

"Hmm, nice," said his dad. "The cool, refreshing taste of Singha, Manchester United's official beer."

"Here son, have a Mister Potato snack – they are the official savoury snack partner of Manchester United."

"What time is it daddy?"

"It's 3:52 and 30 seconds," said his dad.

"That's very precise dad!"

"I can be that precise, thanks to Bulova, United's official timekeeping partner." His dad shook his wrist to accentuate his shiny watch.

It was time to squeeze into their seats. Soon the game began. The passionate crowd swayed from side to side, the noise incredible. The opposition team looked petrified. It was an honour for them to be playing in this cathedral of football, but for now their only concern was repelling wave after wave of incessant attacks from the red-shirted heroes.

They couldn't resist for long though. No one ever could.

Rio Ferdinand swept the ball majestically out of defence. It landed perfectly at the feet of Ryan Giggs. The crowd gasped in anticipation. You could hear a pin drop. Giggsy shimmied inside, passed it to Clevs, who fizzed an inch-perfect pass to Wellsy, who back-heeled it to the rampaging "little pea". He dinked a delightful reverse ball into the box, which was headed on by Roo. The crowd knew what was coming next.

He rose like a salmon. A manicured, tanned salmon, with gel in its gills. Some say he was on the edge of the area. Others say he was 30 yards out. Many will swear that on that fateful day, he headed the ball in from his own half.

The crowd rose as one. Cameras flashed, badges were kissed. The ball hit the back of the goal with such force that the netting was ripped from its moorings, the woodwork close to collapse.

The stadium announcer was close to tears.

"Van Persieeeeeeeee!!!!"

Two minutes later, more of the same.

Ashley Young soared beautifully, ten feet into the air, before crashing back down to earth. A triple pike. Forward roll. Reverse somersault. Full salko.

Penalty. No doubt about that.

Rooney took the ball. The opposition keeper tried to save it, but he knew it was a futile gesture. 2-0.

The crowd rose as one to salute the best-player-in-the-world-except-Messi as he milked the adoration flowing down from the capacity crowd inside this majestic theatre of football.

The ball was zipped around the pitch with a mystical majesty. The opposition players couldn't get close. They huffed and they puffed, but all in vain. They knew they couldn't compete with this amazing collection of players. Some of them couldn't even see the ball, such was the speed it was moved from player to player, from flank to flank. This was how the team always played, as it was in their DNA, part of their glorious history, some other guff, blah blah.

Wayne Rooney was given offside, and he joked with the linesman's assistant as he politely enquired as to whether he thought he had made the correct decision. The linesman's assistant replied that he thought he had, everyone laughed and continued about their business.
The United fans sang songs for the full 90 minutes, and for many hours after too. They were songs about their proud history, and their great players, and that night in Barcelona, and none about Manchester City because they were irrelevant and City fans sang songs about United on the rare occasion they made a noise because they were all obsessed and liars.

The vanquished manager David Moyes walked meekly into Sir Alex's office. A glass of Chateauneuf du Pape awaited him.
"Sorry I am late, was just doing some interviews."
"I don't. They disrespected me once. Get that wee drink down ya, make the day feel a bit better."
SIR Alex laughed heartily.
Moyes took a sip.
"You were magnificent today. We were lucky to only concede eight. You're definitely the best team I have ever seen, you will dominate the game for many years to come. I also love the way you give youth a chance and play football in the right way. You are everything that is right about football."
"Aye, that's kind words indeed, We try our best. I like to stick to my Socialist principles."
"I'm just glad we only have to play you twice a season!"
Both managers laughed until their noses went purple, and agreed that United really were the best team ever...
"David, I'm sorry I had to put your fine Everton team through such an ordeal. I need a wee favour though."
"Anything sir. Just name it."
"You see, I want to be remembered as the best."
"No danger of that not being the case!" exclaimed Moyes, as he looked on with awe.
"Hold on, son. I want more than the trophies. I want my achievements to be realised AFTER I leave. For them to be rammed home to everyone, week by week. I want everyone to realise just how good I was and teach a few that are still here a damn good lesson."
"I see. And how do I come into all of this?"
"Well, it's funny you should say that. How do you fancy a change of scenery?"

And so it began...

Little Eric had a huge smile on his face.
"That's a great story, dad. I hope I can play for United one day!"
His father forced a smile.
"To be honest son, that shouldn't be too difficult..."

"So what happened after that. Did the legacy live on, like the big man Eamonn Holmes said?"

"Well that's a story for another time son. Maybe when you're a bit older, eh?"

"Ok dad!"

The father kissed his son on his forehead and tucked him into bed. He would sleep well with his head full of tales of derring-do. As he slipped out of the room, he turned off the light. But as he went to put the book away, he felt the need to see what did happen after that.

He sat down in his favourite chair with a single malt and opened the book.

EPILOGUE

It had been a tough six months for David Moyes. Another Monday morning had drawn round and he had no intention of reading the papers after United's gritty 1-1 draw at home to Hull City. Reluctantly he dragged himself out of bed and went downstairs. There was a solitary letter on the doormat.

He opened it tentatively. It was from Sir Alex Ferguson. His heart skipped a beat. There was no message, but simply a poem, on the finest quality paper. As he wandered, dazed, into the kitchen, he began to read.

If you can keep your head when all about you
Are losing theirs and blaming it on you,
If you can trust yourself when all men doubt you,
But make allowance for their doubting too;
If you can wait for three points and not be tired by waiting,
Or being lied about, don't deal in lies,
Or being hated, don't give way to hating,
And yet don't look any good, nor talk too wise:

If you can dream of 4th place—and not make dreams your master;
If you can think of winning a game—and not make thoughts of winning two your aim;
If you can meet with Young and Anderson
And treat those two impostors just the same;
If you can bear to hear the inspirational team-talks you've spoken
Twisted by the press to make a trap for fools,
Or watch the things you gave your life to, broken,
And stoop and build 'em up with worn-out tools:

If you can make one heap of all your 7th place winnings
And risk it on one turn of cross-and-head,
And lose (of course), and start again at your beginnings
And never breathe a word about your losses;
If you can force your heart and nerve and sinew
To serve your owners long after they are gone,
And so hold on when there is nothing in you
Except Phil Neville who says to them: 'Hold on!'

If you can talk with dwindling crowds and keep your virtue,
Or walk with Glazers—nor lose the common touch,

If neither City nor every other visiting team can hurt you,
If all men count the crosses with you, but none too much;
If you can fill the unforgiving, depressing final minute
With sixty seconds' worth of distance run,
Yours is the Earth and every sponsorship deal that's in it,
And—which is more—you'll be a Man United manager, my son!

David rested his head against the fridge door. A solitary tear rolled down his cheek and dropped to the floor.

With only the sound of the fridge buzzing and his own heavy breath, he whispered;

"You b**ard Alex. You b***ard."

Open Letters, eh? One of the worst by-products of fans having a voice, here's the second (and third) one in this book, but again, they're obviously not serious.

An Open Letter To Ed Woodward

Dear Ewar Woowar,
Because I am exasperated and a bit needy I am writing this open letter to you that you will never read, because you don't spend your days trawling United message boards reading about fans slagging you off, but I'm doing it anyway as I consider myself overly-important and a voice for the fans.
Right now United fans are feeling raw. We feel dazed and confused. We feel a sense of freedom also, but there are thoughts swimming round our heads and questions we need answering. I hope you will take the time to answer them and don't have to jet off somewhere on some urgent-but-ultimately-futile transfer business.
My first feeling is one of disappointment. You see, United don't sack managers. Yes there was Wilf McGuinness. Yes, I guess there was Ron Atkinson too. Look, I know 3 of United's last 7 permanent managers have been dismissed within 19 months, but that was different – their positions were untenable. United had to act unlike the United way.
As Ollie Holt said the other day:
Manchester United made the right decision when they sacked David Moyes. But they lost something, too.
They lost a big part of their identity. They lost their sense of separateness. It was a separateness that was built on a lot more than just being English football's pre-eminent force for the last 20 years.
So United have lost what set them apart. Now they are just like all the rest.
Managers will come and go every couple of years .Like they do at Chelsea. Like they do at Manchester City.
When they sacked Moyes, United lost their adherence to permanence and checked into the asylum.
Perhaps if he had stayed for another couple of years, a fans' dream team of Gary Neville and caretaker boss Ryan Giggs would have been able to take charge.
Those two understand instinctively what makes a club like United tick in a way that Moyes never did.
Now may be just too soon for them to take it on a permanent basis but if they are given an opportunity after Moyes' successor has come and gone, maybe the idea of a United dynasty can be revived.
The vision, surely, would be a Giggs-Gary Neville spearhead, with Paul Scholes, Nicky Butt and Phil Neville backing them up.

That's the new boot-room. And that could last.
Until then, it's the lucky dip.

OLLIE GETS IT, ED.

Or take Paul Hayward:
There is a Manchester United way, based on attacking, creativity, domination, spirit. Ferguson once said: "I never picked a team without thinking I was going to win the game." The opponent was a dartboard, especially at Old Trafford, where the badge,

the history and the will of the crowd were all harnessed to maintain a domineering mindset.

And then there are the rumours. A club of United's size always generate rumours of course, and their global appeal just fans the flames. But can you please confirm the following rumours to be false:

At one team meeting, Giggs lost his patience with Moyes, shouting "this is a waste of time!" before grabbing Robin Van Persie's house keys and storming out of the training ground. He didn't return until the following day, looking dishevelled.

Is Alex Ferguson really helping choose the next manager? When I once worked at Wetherspoons I convinced the manager to put a boiled egg, cabbage and cow brain stew on the menu. I was never allowed anywhere near the kitchen again.

This is the man who recommended Alex McLeish to Aston Villa. The man is clearly taking the ****.

Are the players backing Giggs as the next manager just so they know where he is? From perusing the media, it appears the Class of 92 have super-powers. What are they?

(I presume Paul Scholes' is invisibility)

Have you got a picture of United's DNA?

Will you just f***ing sign Wesley Sneijder?!

Is it true Toni Kroos had a picture of Neil Webb on his bedroom wall as a nipper?

Was Moyes' biggest mistake was not understanding the United way? Barcelona might style itself as "more than a club", but United are "more than a club than the club that are more than a club" and I think Moyes struggled to grasp this. Gary Neville once commented that United was not a physical entity but more a concept and a state of mind, but I feel he was rather understating the case.

They are of course a plc, but this could easily mean prudence:legends:class.
Privileged, loved, cult.
Poborsky, Law, Cleverley.

United, said Neville, rallied against modern football and all it stood for. They were hipsters before hipsters were invented and they had style and elegance before the sport itself knew the meaning of the words. "More soul than a Motown nightclub," Matt Busby once said of his beloved club.
He knew.
He understood.
He got it.
Will our next manager GET IT? The United way? The DNA?
Under Ferguson, every player understood this, however crap they were. Even Anderson.
Now, the players seem bewildered. Phil Jones looks frightened and confused.
So basically, sort yourself out. We didn't sign up to this. I'm supporting FCUM in the meantime.

<u>An Open Letter To Ed Woodward from A City Fan.</u>

I am writing to express my disgust at your rather impetuous decision to sack David Moyes this week. This is a decision that has saddened and angered me for a number of reasons:

1)   I thought your club gave managers a chance. It's in your DNA and all that. Thus, by removing David Moyes from his post you have ripped the soul from the club and undermined your founding fathers' principles. To make matters worse, you have upset Ollie Holt – he thought you were better than this.

2)   By getting rid of David Moyes, there is now a realistic possibility that United will be managed by someone who knows what he is doing. This worries me.

3)   Thirdly, and this is by far the most important point: a couple of months ago my friends and I grouped together to purchase a banner honouring United's new manager. I have enclosed a picture below.

As you can see, a lot of thought went into the design and a fair bit of money too. Banners are not cheap, as Tufty will tell you (the ****). Anyway, we favoured this particular design because we felt it was a banner that would be relevant for years to come. Safe in the knowledge that United are a class above any other club and that it is part of your soul, your essence, your being, that you give managers time, we went ahead with the purchase. With a six-year contract handed to Mr Moyes, we were confident that he would see this contract out – that's the United way. It thus seemed a safe investment, and we looked forward to upping the number with each passing year.

You can imagine my surprise this morning then when news emerged of David Moyes being close to the sack. At first I dismissed it as spurious media-stirring, but then the news broke that it was all true and the chosen one had gone.

I am, quite frankly, disgusted.

I'll get to the point – you owe me £300. The banner is now worthless, and I hold Manchester United wholly responsible for this. How do you intend to rectify the situation? Would a cheque payable to me be acceptable?

Please let me know of your intentions at the soonest opportunity. I look forward to corresponding with you and rectifying this unfortunate situation. After consultation with my friends I am willing to accept the offer of helping choose your next manager as an alternative form of compensation, or at least a coffee with you Ed to pass on some of my thoughts.

Regards.
Harold Hodgkin
P.S. Would you be interested in taking the banner off our hands to display in your museum?

Football In The Bible: Part 2

Genesis & Exodus

In the beginning there was earth and Sepp Blatter.

Now the whole world had one language and a common speech, and this language was football. As people moved eastward, and westward they found a tax haven in Zurich and settled there.

But the LORD came down to see the people. "Come, let us go down and confuse their language so they will not understand each other." And thus some called it soccer and some picked up a squashed ball and called that football.
So the LORD scattered them from there over all the earth, even to Qatar.

They said to each other, "Come, let us build ourselves a city, with two towers that reach to the heavens, so that we may make a name for ourselves; otherwise we will be scattered over the face of the whole earth." And this was Wembley.
And great rivers of urine would flow down the aisles during competition.

And the LORD added, as he was a chatterbox and a bit lonely: "As for you, be fruitful and increase in number; multiply on the earth and increase upon it."

And one woman named Jordan did take this command seriously, and she did multiply and she begat many men.
And Dwight of York(e) did make an eventful journey through Jordan.

When Yorke was 25 years old, he became the father of Harvey. And after he became the father of Harvey, Yorke lived 100 years and had other sons and daughters and begat many women of glamour.

When Jordan had lived 24 years, she became the mother of Harvey. And after she became the mother of Harvey, Jordan lived forever and had other sons and daughters.

But first she begat Teddy from the town of London, and Dane of Bowers, who was on another level. Then she begat Warren the gladiator, who was ace.
And the LORD did proclaim: "Awooga."

When Jordan had lived 27 years, she became the mother of Junior Savva Andreas Andre having previously begat Gareth at the heavenly gates and Peter of Andre. And after she became the mother of Junior Savva Andreas Andre, Jordan lived forever and had other sons and daughters.

When Jordan had lived 30 years, she became the mother of Princess Tiaamii Crystal Esther Andre having previously begat Alex Reid and Peter of Andre. And after she became the mother of Princess Tiaamii Crystal Esther Andre, Jordan lived forever and had other sons and daughters.

When Jordan had lived 33 years, she became the mother of Jett Riviera having previously begat Leandro Penna and Peter of Andre. And after she became the mother of Jett Riviera, Jordan lived forever and had other sons and daughters.

When Jordan had lived 36 years, she became the mother of Chardonnay Dame Butternut S'quash Bianca Precious Price having previously begat Kieran Hayler and Peter of Andre. And after she became the mother of Chardonnay Dame Butternut S'quash Bianca Precious Price, Jordan lived forever and had other sons and daughters.

And after naming her 5th child, the lord did ask "Are you ******* serious?" and Jordan doth reply "yes I am." And so it was thus.

Yet whilst Jordan populated the earth and spread the seed, a tribe with no history sought refuge and a place to stay two thousand and three years after Christ.

The LORD'S cityzens did say unto him, thou shalt build me a council house to dwell in: for I have dwelt in a mis-shaped house since the day that I brought up the blues unto this day. And I sat on uncovered seats and I was wet.
The lord spaketh: I will ordain a place for my people, and will plant them, and they shall dwell in their place, and shall be moved no more, except for European games and stadium expansions;

And a man named Bernstein did predict: He shall build me a house, and I will establish his throne for ever, and due to a market-fair sponsorship deal, it shall be named the Etihad.

Bernstein travelled through the land as far as the site of the great tree of Beswick. The LORD appeared to Bernstein and said, "To your offspring I will give this land." So he built an altar there to the LORD, who had appeared to him and he called it the B of the Bang. But it did fall apart and speared three people, so it was destroyed by fire and cranes and rust.

Now there was a famine in the land, and the people did not see a single goal for months. So Stuart of Pearce brought forth Beanie and he did see an upturn in fortune and all did rejoice, occasionally.

And out of the wilderness came three wise men.

These wise men brought gifts. Gold, Frank's (in cents) share of the club and more.

And the lord did apologise for the previous line. And the three wise men were Sheikh Mansour, Khaldoon al Mubarak, and a joker whose name the LORD has forgotten who was soon despatched to the shimmering deserts of the east.

There was great joy amongst the cityzens and this joy was purchased with petrodollars. But it was non-organic joy and this provoked wrath in others.

But then the red tribe came to the fore with the greatest attacking threat seen since the birth of the glorious game, which was a thousand years and nine hundred and

ninety years with two more years after Christ. #ynwa
1992. I'm trying to say 1992. Why didn't people talk normal in those days?

But the author did digress. Then the LORD said to the cityzens, "Why are you angry? Why is your face downcast? You must believe." And the Lord did log into Twitter and create the believe hashtag, and so it was that it was trending in Manchester, as was #fighttotheend, #mercenaryyaya and #sellgarciai'lldrivehimtotheairportmyselfififihaveto.

And a great man led the tribe to greatness, and he was named Stevie G. And the people spake on the mount, saying that glory was his destiny and fitting, in this year of all years. But with magnificent spoils in sight he did slip and the man of sheep did take the ball and place it firmly in the onion bag. #ynwa

And Stevie G spake to the lord, for he was distressed and he said:
Hear me, lest otherwise they should rejoice over me: when my foot slippeth, they magnify themselves against me. For I am ready to halt, and my sorrow is continually before me. For I will declare mine iniquity; I will be sorry for my sin.
But mine enemies are lively, and they are strong: and they that hate me wrongfully are multiplied and have fine voice when signing songs about me.
Make haste to help me, O Lord my salvation

And the tribe walked on, and they walked on, with no hope in their hearts, and the bus that was without roof did reverse into the garage, and there was much beeping and there was also much weeping and silences of sixty seconds at the surrender #ynwa

But the messiah spoke to his people and he did say: "People, we made a great journey. This year I doth hand out no envelopes, as our warriors did capture the hearts of a nation, and of all neutrals. From Newcastle, which is by the brink of the river of Tyne, and from the city that is by the river, even unto Birmingham, there was not one city too strong for us: the LORD our God delivered all unto us: except for the crystal palace. And Chelsea. And the cityzens of Manchester. And I proclaim now – next year will definitely be our year." #ynwa

And lo(l), they captured Ricky Lambert #ynwa

And there was sadness around the land, in studios from the north to the south, from the west to the east. From the Lawrenson tribe to the Hansen tribe to the Rush tribe to the Thompson tribe to the Owen tribe to the Fowler tribe to the Redknapp tribe to the Hamann tribe to the Reade tribe to the Green tribe – across the land a great sorrow spread like pestilence and consumed all those in suits of shells #ynwa.

And the chosen one brought the united tribe out of Europe with a mighty hand. And thus he was exiled to the wilderness as united aspired to be like the cityzens. In exile was where he did fight in wine bars. And he did transgresseth by wine, as was the United manager way.

And into exile followed Micah, Les'cott and the milliner and Rod'well.

And there was great mourning and anger at the Daily Mail, as Neil of Ashton asked what this meant for the country's team. And he thought it was bad.

The Book of Figures

But then a great cloud covered the east of Manchester, a plague sent from the east. And the lord did say:
I send a curse, if ye will not obey the commandments of UEFA your god, but turn aside out of the way which I command you this day.

For if ye shall diligently keep all these commandments which I command you, to do them, to love the UEFA your God, to walk in all his ways, and to cleave unto him; then will the LORD drive out all these penalties from before you, and ye shall possess greater solvency.

And ye shall observe to do all the statutes and judgments which I set before you this day, for these commandments have come from above, from David of Gill, from David of Dein from Arsene of Wenger and from Karl Heinz of Rumenigge. For they doth protect their interests at your expense and it must be so for these are the rules.

For the wicked plotteth against the just, and gnasheth upon him with his teeth, saying financial fair play is just. The sheikh did laugh at him, for he seeth that his day is coming.

The wicked G14 have drawn out the sword, and have bent their bow, to cast down the poor and needy, and to slay such as be of upright conversation. Their sword shall enter into their own heart, and their bows shall be broken. And the red devils, led astray into the wilderness by the chosen one, shall reap what they sow. The wicked borroweth via debt and leverage and payeth not again: but the righteous showeth mercy and giveth, both in trophies and pukka pies and city square and holistic ways.

The Book of Bumps

And Brian of Marwood hastened into the tent unto Sarah the lady of the canteen, and said, make ready quickly three measures of fine meal, knead it, and make cakes upon the hearth. For it be Yaya's birthday and thou hast forgotten amidst the celebrating of the great title. Go forth and knead, for he is needy.

And they gave him a piece of a cake of figs, and two clusters of raisins: and when he had eaten, his spirit came again to him: for he had eaten no bread, nor drunk any water, three days and three nights. Nor had he been sung to nor even had the bumps. And he was not happy as he felt unloved. And he went to his advisor and he did tell him to arrange him an escape.

Then Mansour said to Kolo, "Where is your brother Yaya?"
"I don't know," he replied. "Am I my brother's keeper?"
The LORD said, "What have you done? Listen! Your brother's agent cries out to me from the ground. Now you are under a curse. You will be a restless wanderer on the earth and be sold to QPR."

Kolo said to Mansour, "My punishment is more than I can bear."
So Kolo went out from the scousers' presence and lived in the land of London, east of Bath. And his keeper Harry, who was inflicted with cockneyness, did proclaim he was triffic.

And the agent said unto Yaya, depart, and go up hence, thou and the people which thou hast brought up out of the land of east Manchester, unto a land flowing with milk and honey: for I will not go up in the midst of thee; for thou art a stiffnecked people with great facial hair: lest I consume thee in the way.

And when the people heard these evil tidings, they mourned: and no man did put on him his ornaments nor on the back of his shirt.

And the people did slate Yaya on Twitter. But then Yaya did backtrack quicker than a Liverpool parade bus and did say he was mistaken as his advisor did find no suitor in the land of Catalans, and the people did worship Yaya once more and they did proclaim: "when you are of thirty and two years, we will not forget. And there will be cakes and balloons and streamers and a party with fish and bread. And so it came to pass, that there was a party with cakes and balloons and streamers and Yaya was happy for another year as he had six hundred extra shekels of gold by weight."

And he said, I beseech thee, shew me thy glory. And the people did shake their hands low and high and did sing him his song.

The Book of Cups

And every four years we shall celebrate this holy kicking of the pig's bladder with a competition. And the lord did command that only certain words would be spaken from competition beginning to competition end, and these words were the best a man can get, always coca-cola and impossible is nothing. Just do it spoke the LORD.

And Wayne Rooney did place the ball into orbit from twelve cubits, and the ball did travel through the heavens for 40 days and 40 nights before landing in Argentina. And Wayne was distraught and appealed for leniency. And he was taken to one side and he was reassured and he was introduced to an ad man from Domino's and everything was peaceful.

And Jesus did feed the five thousand. And he did walk on water. And he did perform many miracles. And great plagues were brought down on the people. And the earth was flooded. And Adam did speak to a snake. And Phil Jones and Chris Smalling and Tom Cleverley did lead England to glory in the competition of each four years. And the LORD did take the author of the bible to one side and he did say "you can't put in that bit about Jones, Smalling & Cleverley, for the people will think the book too far-fetched." And thus the author did replace their story of glory with a tale about the sea parting in two.

Book of Epilogues

The steps of a good man are ordered by the Lord: and he delighteth in his way.

He is ever merciful, and lendeth; and his seed is blessed. He is Vincent Kompany.

Depart from evil, and do good; and dwell for evermore said the lord, and he did so.

The lord spake: the righteous shall inherit the land, and dwell therein for ever, or at least until the tenancy expires.

And the rest, as the LORD did say, was history.....

Commentators: Much Ado About Nothing

Commentators. I have a theory about them – a theory which basically states that Kenneth Wolstenholme has got a lot to answer for and it's entirely his fault that I dislike so many of the current crop of those who comment on the beautiful game..

Wolstenholme's "they think it's all over" quote from the 1966 World Cup final was a spur of the moment comment that gained international fame, book deals, was sampled in hit records and even got its own TV show.

Wolstenholme had previously been established as the BBC's authoritative voice of football and went on to cover the climax of five World Cup championships and the finals of 16 European Cups and 23 FA Cup finals besides dozens of internationals. He was proud that he had produced a timeless piece of broadcasting and coined a phrase that has entered English folklore. But this was tinged with a hint of regret that the words had overshadowed the rest of a hugely successful and ground-breaking career (though he used the phrase for title of his memoirs, so wasn't too upset, clearly).

Over on ITV, Hugh Johns was the "the other voice" of the 1966 World Cup final. At the same moment, to a much smaller audience, Mr Johns was concentrating more on the striker's hat-trick as he told ITV viewers: "Here's Hurst, he might make it three. He has! He has… so that's it. That is IT!"

I like Johns' commentary. It does the job for me. The problem is no one remembers his words. And now every commentator does not want his Johns moment, but his Wolstenholme moment. It seems sometimes that every commentator wants fame and a legacy of a piece of beautiful prose at a key moment in a key match. And no Clive Tyldesley, anything to do with "that night in Barcelona" doesn't count. So rather than comment on what's happening on the pitch, commentaries have become a competition to see who can say the most dramatic, prose-soaked comment. I am still scarred by a Portsmouth match commentated on by Peter Drury a few seasons gone, where Drury felt it apt to continuously refer to Portsmouth's financial problems by quoting Shakespeare. It was the best of times, and it was the worst of times, you see!

Oh hang on, that's Dickens.

But as Piquione volleyed in the second goal, I thought to myself that it was a far, far better thing that he did, than I have ever done; and I couldn't help think that it was a far, far better rest that he went to than I have ever known.
Drury would have worded it so much better though.
"What can Portsmouth do in this second half? If football be the food of love, play on. To sleep, perchance, to dream, for the Pompey fans have discovered that all that glitters is not gold. O coward conscience, how dost thou afflict me, and Utaka's missed an absolute sitter there! Lord, what fools these mortals be. Thoughts, Craig Burley?"
"Well, youse got to say he should've buried that, the lad's gonna be disappointed not to hit the target."

A new breed of commentators emerged a few years ago, each of whom seemed to have their own "angle". Commentating well was deemed not to be sufficient anymore.

For Drury this meant prose and intellectual nonsense, Alan Green's was to criticise everything, and Jonathan Pearce's "angle" was to SHOUT VERY LOUDLY about everything, because even a throw-in early in the game had its own little frisson. Stick to Robot Wars Jonathan.

Now I have no problem with commentators doing research before a match – they should be doing, it's their job, not that this has concerned studio pundits or many co-commentators. What I can't stand is the need to crowbar statistics in and more than that, the need to crowbar puns and catchphrases that they have been working on, as if they have just completed a six-week tabloid headline-writing course.

Jonathan Pearce has said that 90% of his job is research, but only 2% of that will be used during a match. That's how it should be. Less is more.

It wasn't all this way – it's easy to get nostalgic, but Davies, the old Motson (by which I mean the young Motson) or Wolstenholme did not attract the ire that their modern counterparts do. Maybe that is just a result of modern media whereby anyone (even me) can broadcast their views to anyone who will listen. All you had in the old days was Barry Took on Points of View.

And then there's Alan Green. It's very fashionable to have a go at Alan Green, so that's what I am going to do.

Now he has his supporters of course, who argue quite simply that he is one of the few commentators to "say it as it is". I am not sure what they mean by this, but presumably, they mean he whinges, moans and criticises everything before him. So in other words, they think football is rubbish. He certainly seems to think so – if he does enjoy the beautiful game, he certainly hides it.

At one Champions League final, for which he was being paid handsomely to watch, his first thought was to moan about how awful the commentary position was.

For an England international, within three minutes of the match kicking off he had moaned about the weather (sorry we couldn't sort that out for you Alan), the new England kit, banners around the edge of the ground (he doesn't like them, like most things), and two attempted tackles/passes by England players.

It's all subjective of course, but even I know there are good commentators. Generally those that stick to describing the action, give you a rounded-picture of the match, and keep matters in perspective. I've no doubt it is not an easy job, but it can be done well. What I don't need to know, because I don't care, is what the commentator thinks about City's wealth, banners around grounds, Mexican waves, football kits, the weather, managers, the price of tuna in supermarkets or the quality of hamburgers at Villa Park. I'll form my own opinions, thanks. You're there to describe the match – I'm well aware tuna is ridiculously expensive nowadays.

But despite Green, radio seems to have got it right more than television. Radio 5's football coverage is generally excellent, and it is TV that seems to struggle. With radio commentary, you are required to stick to the script and describe what is happening, as you are the eyes. With TV, commentators seem to think that silence is evil, and must not be allowed. I couldn't disagree more. You could turn the sound off, but then you'd lose crowd noise too.

So I would argue that the memorable moments, on and off the pitch are spontaneous moments that cannot be rehearsed and planned in advance. Going back to that glorious day, and it got me wondering how Drury would have covered that 1966 World Cup Final finale.

"And here comes Hurst, sprinting up the pitch. Could this be it? Geoff Hurst, ask not what England will do for you, but what together we can do for the freedom of man! Let every nation know, whether it wishes us well or ill, that we shall pay any price, bear any burden, meet any hardship, support any friend, oppose any foe, in order to assure the survival and the success of liberty! Goal!"

As for Alan Green?

Green: *"Some people are on the pitch. Oh this is disgusting, absolute disgrace. Ban them for life, no one wants to see this, animals, what are they thinking, shame on you, shame on you! I am embarrassed to be British, this is shocking, are they looking for a fight, they might be, idiots, absolute idiots, oh dear oh dear, ruined the game for me, shocking."*

Jimmy Armfield: *"Hurst has scored by the way, 4-2, hat trick for him, England have won the World Cup!"*

Green: *"Have they? Oh but it's been overshadowed for me, it really has…oh, and now everyone's doing a Mexican wave, they really should be shot. Lamentable."*

Hugh Johns had the right idea.

Football's Worst Cliches.

It's in the club's DNA
Apparently certain football clubs are genetically designed to play football a certain way. That way is always the same of course – free-flowing, attacking football. You won't hear a commentator comment on how it's in a club's DNA to play dour, plodding football. Often, the genetic need to play attractive football is because the fans "demand it", because you see many fans of other clubs are happy to watch tedious long-ball football week-in, week-out, whilst over at Old Trafford or Upton Park, to quote but two random examples, there are often riots in the streets over something as trivial as a back-pass to the keeper. In fact, there is a theory that the summer riots of 2011 began after Sam Allardyce changed to a defensive 4-5-1 formation during a game against Stoke City.
Quoting a few of your flair players from the 60's and 70's is usually sufficient to prove that your club does things differently to the masses. It may also be in a club's DNA to "never give in", "fight to the end" which may be linked to a club DNA that means plenty of last-minute winners. I'm not naming any names. #MU

The club's soul
There is no such thing as a soul and even if there was, football clubs would not possess one. So shut up Ollie Holt.

The ball moved in the air
Always helpful when playing football, I find.

He hit it too well.
No. No, he didn't. This is not possible.

The keeper shouldn't be beaten at his near post
I've no idea why a keeper's near post is treated as a no-man's land. It seems letting the ball past your near post is worse than waving it inside the far post.

I've seen them given
My personal favourite and the go-to place for the inept co-commentator who can't decide if it should be a penalty or not after 17 slow-motion replays from 6 separate angles. If you hear this from a co-commentator you can safely assume it was not a penalty.

He's not that type of player
Yes, he did fly in too-footed and snap that player's leg in half, before punching three of the opposition team, spitting at the referee, attacking the 4th official with the injury-time board before finally urinating on a member of the crowd.
But he's not that type of player.

Collector's Item
A good player screws a shot wide, and yet again we are subjected to the comment that the miss was a collector's item, or maybe one for the scrapbook. I've seen Messi shoot wide 100 times.

(Co-) Commentator – "A late flag there."
So?
I don't care if he puts it up immediately, 2 seconds later, twirls his flag in the air before doing a somersault with triple pike, followed by the splits and finishing off with his own unique rendition of Gerry Rafferty's "Baker Street", ably assisted by the Royal Philharmonic's saxophone section before moon walking up the touchline and high-fiving the fourth official. All I care about is that he gets the decision right. What is of less importance is that the linesman raises his flag within 0 .6 of a second.

"It was a good time to score."
Because there's nothing worse than seeing your team score between the 20th and 30th minute – I mean, what's the point?

It was a stonewall penalty
Time for "pedantry corner". This makes no sense. Surely it should be stone-cold? And even that doesn't make great sense. What's wrong with nailed-on eh?

Teams are at their most vulnerable after they've scored.
I have no stats to back this up, but I will say it anyway – what a load of c**p.

"It's a red card, but I just wish, for the sake of entertainment, that referees used common sense sometimes."
Shut up.

There was contact.
Fancy that, what with football being a contact sport and all that. Well it used to be anyway....

"It doesn't matter who you draw in the cup – you've got to beat the best sides to win it..."
What sort of mind cannot comprehend the randomness of a cup draw, or the fact that you can get to a final without meeting many top sides, or that meeting a good side in every round somewhat diminishes your chances of going all the way?

"A great shot there.." (for any shot that goes wide)

No shot that goes wide is a great shot. This is a fact. Cut it out co-commentators.

Sir Alex & The Theatre of Nightmares

This story is entirely fictional. Names have nevertheless been changed(again) to protect the guilty.

Sir Alex Fergusan and Mick Hucknell were not happy. Not happy at all. In fact, both had visibly aged since Luis Suarez had popped in the sixth goal.

The club was going through a rough patch, no doubt about that. Club ambassador Wayne Roaney had been photographed leaving Sandy's Superstars again, and then there was Bryn Robson….
Roaney had told Alex he was only there to promote Red Bull, United's official senior members' energy drink partner for Europe, Indo-China and Bali, but he was fooling no-one.

Alex was back in charge, but it wasn't the same. Mick was his right-hand man, there to gee up the players and sing at half-time. Holding Back The Years had been beautifully performed during the break against Chelsea, but it hadn't prevented a 4-0 defeat. What's more, Ryan Gigs had started crying mid-chorus.
Difficult times.

"Pass-and-move, the Liverpool groove" was number one in the download charts as the team from Anfield swept all before them apart from the odd team above them in the table. They were back on their bloody perch again, though their fans kept their counsel and rarely gloated. At that precise moment, #ynwa was trending in Cork, Belfast and also the Wirral.

David Moyles had since moved to Bayern Munich, who were now in a desperate relegation fight. The players were disinterested, to the point that Arjen Robbin didn't even bother diving anymore. To make matters worse, Phil Nevelle and Franck Ribenary had scuffled on the training pitch, causing no extra facial damage whatsoever. Moyles hadn't helped matters by commenting that Bayern Munich aspired to be like Borussia Dortmund.

Moyles had fought to keep his job at United, but couldn't fight the tide forever. After a brave 1-1 performance against Juventus, Moyles had stormed into the dressing room and torn his shirt off, before emitting a guttural roar. Having adorned himself with face paints and trashed the warm-down area, his players knew the end was near. He was later found eating a Toblerone in his car at Birch Services. "*CHOSEN GONE!*" screamed the Daily Mirror the following day.

He had been replaced by Lewis Van Gawl, whose reign started with him punching the journalist Olly Hoult in his first press conference after Hoult asked him about United's soul and DNA. It was downhill from there, and after Van Gawl was found holding Tim Cleverley's head under water in the team bath after a 3-0 home defeat to West Brom, his days were also numbered, especially as the previous week he had put Darren Fletcher in goal for a penalty-shoot out in the Capital One Cup. IN the end he dropped his shorts in a press conference and slapped journalist Neal Custis about the face with his John Thomas, and that was that. Mutual consent said the board, but everyone knew otherwise.

And so Alex was back, but it wasn't the same. Games ended after 92/3 minutes, referees weren't scared of him and even the BBC were now ignoring him.

And then there was Madchester Citeh. Alex and Mick had once reminisced about a pre-season tour to Malaysia, when over 2 million people had come to watch one training session alone.
Alex chuckled as he recalled a particular taxi ride in Kuala Lumpur, when the driver kept shouting "Bobby Charlton!" at them and told them no one knew who Madchester City were. The taxi driver thought Alex was making them up! Happy days.

Not happy days anymore. City were holistic, and kept winning trophies. The oil hadn't run out and they had a new shiny academy. They had new legions of fans, and some of them didn't even have moustaches. Their income kept going up and up and it wouldn't be long until they too had an official milkshake partner for the Benelux region. They had no history, but they were very noisy neighbours, no doubt about that.

There was still plenty of things to be positive about though. Adrian Januzaj was so good that United had stopped playing him to try and prevent Real Madrid buying him. Now that United played at the Nike Superdome, there was a bit of money in the war-chest. United had a £75m a year totally-market-fair kit deal with Adidas and were selling endless kits. But they needed to win some trophies again, to be at the top, hovering up the best players through organically earned money and lording it voer everyone else. It was in their DNA, the United way.

Alex returned home, tired and deflated. As he opened the front door, he noticed a slip of paper on the mat, folded in half. Intrigued, he opened it outwards and read what was scribbled on the sheet:

Hi Alex, it's me David Moyles. Hope you are well gaffer. Remember that poem you once sent me? The one to gee me up when times were tough? Well I thought it only fair to return the favour, so this is for you. I hope you like it and I hope it gets you through these difficult times:

Stop all the clocks, cut off the telephone,
Prevent the dog from barking with a juicy bone,
Silence Boyley and with muffled drum
Bring out the Capital One Cup 2nd Round draw, let the mourners come.

Let aeroplanes circle moaning overhead
Scribbling on the sky the message: Moyes Out Football Is Dead,
Put green and yellow bows round the necks of the public droves,
Let the stewards wear black Adidas cotton gloves.

United was my North, my South, my East and West,
My working week and my Super Sunday best,

My noon, my midnight, my talk, my Monty Python song;
I thought that love would last for ever (subject to continued success and sensible
ownership that promoted organic growth and reinvested profits in buying all the best
players so that the trophies kept coming): I was wrong.

The B-list stars are not wanted now: sell or loan every one;
Pack up the moon and dismantle the sun;
Pour away the ocean's finance and sweep up the deadwood.
For nothing now can ever come to any good.

Seven miles away a man sat in his garden, soaking up the last remnants of the summer sun. Suddenly, his ears pricked and his head swivelled to his right and he thought to himself, *"was that a screaming man I just heard?"*

He couldn't be sure.

Random Tweets From Recent Years

Ian McGarry: Seven points clear to eight points behind. I very much doubt that Sheikh Mansour will forgive Mancini and retain him as coach.

Terry Christian: our tradition of exciting attacking football is an example to the world and every stride by a man in red is a moral victory.

Oliver Holt: Ok, ok, I know City fans think I banged on too much about Mark Hughes but irrespective of that, surely you deserve better than Mancini.

Manchester United coach Rene Meulendteen, April 2012: "Manchester City don't have a well-balanced team. They only have individuals who play for themselves. You can see that they lack the right team spirit.
"There's no chance of Balotelli playing for Manchester United - a player who gets up to the sort of antics he does has no place at our club. I don't believe Sir Alex would sign a player like Balotelli."

After Arsenal beat Manchester City: John Cross: "If Sunday told us anything, The Emirates is a happier place for Van Persie to be. "

John Barnes: "I believe what's going to happen now is that players won't stay at clubs for so long, especially the foreign players. What Sir Alex Ferguson and Kenny Dalglish are doing is signing players they think will stay for years. Phil Jones, Ashley Young, Stewart Downing and Charlie Adam, they're not going to be looking to move anywhere else. Look at City now with Tevez, and what you get with foreign players who really have no allegiance to the club."

Pete Gill, football365.com : "City, reborn by a cash rejection from a man who has only seen them play twice in person, are a club without history."

Martin Samuel: If Phil Jones impresses in midfield he has the capability to change the English game in the way Desailly changed France.

Ollie Holt: Aguero will be highest profile signing of summer.. still think Charlie Adam to Liverpool could be best though.

Martin Lipton: Aguero is a gamble, and the wrong man to replace Tevez.

Ollie Holt: Is it acceptable then to change name of team, too? Presuming all in favour of Etihad Stadium would be fine with Etihad City as name of team?

MUTV Listings

08:00: Last of the Summer Whine – Listen live as United's manager criticises the fixture list.

09:00: Bargain Hunt: Ed Woodward desperately tries to find value in the market.

09:40: Through The Keyhole – hosted by Martin Edwards.

10:45: Top Gear. Watch as <name removed for legal reasons> misses a random drug test.

11:30: Celebrity Fit Club: On this week's show, Kolo, a car salesman from Liverpool, tries to shed the pounds, with hilarious consequences.

11:45: UKIP Party Political Broadcast – Guest speaker David Moyes explains why it is best being out of Europe.

~~12:22: Champions League Highlights~~

13:00: Homes Under The Hammers – The Story of West Ham's move to the Olympic Stadium.

13:45: Fifteen To One: The story of Manchester United's transfer business in the summer of 2013, as their targets are slowly whittled down to Marouane Fellaini.

14:00: Grand Designs. This week, David Moyes tells MUTV how United aspire to be like Manchester City.

14:30: Countdown: The story of Manchester United's transfer business in the summer of 2013, as their targets are slowly whittled down to Marouane Fellaini.

15:00: Absolutely Fabulous – A profile of the greatest young player in the world – Adnan Januzaj.

15:25: Jackanory – Sean Custis & Ian Herbert gather in the studio to discuss United's big summer transfer targets, just ahead of the season ticket renewal date.

15:45: Embarrassing Bodies – Wayne Rooney returns to pre-season training.

16:30: Family Guy: A documentary on Ryan Giggs.

17:00: You've Been Framed: Alex Ferguson is persuaded to sign Bebe instead of James Rodriguez (see also: Rogue Traders).

17:45: Deal or No Deal: A documentary charting United's attempts to sign Wesley Sneijder.

18:30: Edge of Darkness – David Moyes takes over the hot-seat at Old Trafford.

19:00: Splash – this week, Tom Daley takes on Ashley Young.

19:25: Home & Away: Another documentary on Ryan Giggs.

20:00: Pop Idol: Wayne Rooney tells MUTV about his favourite fizzy drinks.

21:00: Comic Relief – a look at Manchester United's 2013/14 campaign.

21:30: Sex & The City: Ryan Giggs takes a turn looking at the 2013/14 campaign from a personal viewpoint.

22:04: Liar Liar: Extracts from Alex Ferguson's autobiography.

22:30: The Last Emperor: A look at Alex Ferguson under the Glazers.

23:00: Brief Encounter: Bobby Charlton allegedly helps you get those elusive match tickets.

23:30: The Trip – Ashley Young explains in a candid interview why he keeps hitting the ground in opposition penalty areas.

00:00: End of transmission: Alex Ferguson shuts down MUTV as they mention in a panel discussion that Phil Jones is weaker on his left foot.

World Cup Review: The Group Stages

The tournament started with a riot of goals and riots in the streets. Protests around social conditions were followed up with protests over Adrian Chiles' presenting skills, which resulted in the studio being pelted with rocks. Welcome to our world, Brazil. Matters came to a head when Chiles presented a show in shorts and flip-flops.

Brazil got the obligatory homer referee for their opening game against Croatia and the goals continued to flow until Iran and Nigeria ruined it all not only by failing to score, but by providing the tournament with its first draw after five days of games.

FIFA themselves were embroiled in scandal, as is their natural state of existence – and as usual they swanned about the host country like royalty. Sepp Blatter was carried around in a sedan chair as specially chosen children from the favelas fanned him with gold-plated coconut leaves, whilst all the FIFA delegates relaxed in 5-star hotels, ate only the finest food and wines known to humanity and took advantage of the many spurious laws that FIFA impose during a world cup competition. These included:

• Sepp Blatter to be addressed at all times as "your excellency".
 • A masseur to follow three steps behind FIFA delegates at all times.
 • Budweiser to be the only alcoholic drink to be consumed by Brazilians during the month of June.
 • The FIFA logo to be projected by laser onto the moon for the duration of the competition.
 • Bendy hot-dogs branded illegal as they went against "the ethos and ideals" of the FIFA family.
 • Set times for tides.
 • A 75ft statue of Sepp Blatter to be erected outside the Maracana made entirely from hardened zero-fat cottage cheese.
 • All team kits to be one matching colour (oh hang on, that one's true)

The truth is not far from that. After all, FIFA has trademarked nearly 200 words and phrases for its exclusive commercial use. However, for once the locals have fought back. Having served up acarajé (a dish made from peeled black-eyed peas formed into a ball and then deep-fried in palm oil) in the old stadium in Salvador for many decades, the sellers were shocked to be excluded from the vendors selected for the new stadium. So they started a high-profile campaign to force FIFA to allow the custom to continue. And they won.
 During the six matches at the stadium, there will be six acarajé sellers on the stadium grounds. A ripple effect from this victory means local customs are now being accommodated in and around World Cup More than 16,000 people signed a petition. Local politicians, stung by the demonstrations, became visibly more careful of local sensitivities. In the city of Recife, eight tapioca sellers (a pancake made from the cassava plant, typically served with cheese, meat, chocolate or fruit) will be based just inside the entrance to the shiny new stadium. Take that FIFA.

It was another horror show in the commentary boxes of Brazil. Jonathan Pearce started it off, struggling to deal with the concept of a ball crossing the goal-line and the use of video technology to show this, the ball crossing the line a central concept of the sport since its birth in the 19th century. Do catch up Jonathan. To make matters worse, after a national outcry and questions asked about his competence in the House of Commons (and on Mumsnet), Pearce exacerbated his error by continuing the theme in his next commentary by continuing to claim that the technology had not worked and had created a controversy.

We should have left him on Robot Wars.

Things weren't much better elsewhere. Some executive had the bright idea of inviting Robbie Savage into the commentary box, where he had a tendency to shout a lot and sound exasperated at every missed pass. Then of course there was Phil Neville, who single-handedly sent a nation to sleep with his vocal cords. He did us all a favour as England succumbed to Italy.

The worst of the lot though, again, was Mark Lawrenson, who in the early days of the tournament seemed to be residing under a canal bridge judging by his on-screen appearance. Eventually he got his s**t together, but once more Mark seemed rather inconvenienced at being paid handsomely to commentate on a match in the Maracana.

The questions over Wayne Rooney's place in the team/fitness/hair provided the most tedious narrative of the campaign, making Wesley Sneijder/Manchester United transfer speculation seem almost exciting in comparison. In the end he was of course ok and nothing more – fancy that.

A knackered-looking Spain bowed out after just two games, their performances so bad they were on the plane home before England. Not long before however, as England limped out after a 2-1 defeat to Uruguay and the world continued to bemoan the lack of Englishmen in City's title-winning squad. In the end, it was the England players' lack of gusto when singing the national anthem that did for them. I mean, there were Ivory Coast players literally crying during their anthem.

Ivory Coast went out in the group stages.

With Harry "honest as the day is long*" Redknapp spreading rumours that some players couldn't even be bothered playing for their country, Ian Wright very sensibly suggested that each of those players should have to phone the parents of a soldier killed in Afghanistan to explain themselves.

"Hi, is that Mrs Smith?"

"Erm, yes.."

"Sorry to bother you, but this is Andros Townsend, I pulled out of an England friendly against Peru last year to be with my heavily-pregnant partner and I'd like to apologise profusely and explain my actions."

"Right..erm..I'm not sure this is really relevant to me, and it's not a good time to be honest...."

"Yes I appreciate that, but I think it a fitting punishment for my indiscretion that I explain to a complete stranger why I did what I did in full and I think it fitting I explain to someone currently grieving who has no interest in football whatsoever..."

"Hello... Mrs Smith...hello..."

There is obviously no downside to this idea, and I can't think of any way it could backfire. I also happen to think the moon is made of cheese and Piers Morgan is a bloody nice chap.
(* an Arctic winter day)

Scapegoats were needed of course for England's abject failure, but on this occasion the choice was too wide to zero in on one person and there were no relevant vegetables to super-impose on Roy Hodgson's head. Thankfully redemption came, and it came in the form of a gritty 0-0 draw with the pre-tournament favourites Costa Rica. The England players could get on that plane back from Rio with their heads held high – the bulldog spirit had shone through and we almost had a penalty. Sadly the passion presented by the players was not replicated back home, a solitary person turning up at the airport to greet our heroes' return, and she may have been waiting for someone else.

City's players haven't had the best of tournaments, Dzeko Mk II out in force for the tournament though he was robbed by yet another incompetent linesman in the game against Nigeria. David Silva looked knackered but Fernandinho took just a couple of minutes to show his manager what the rest of the world already knew – he's a tad better than Paulinho. By the end of the match against Cameroon, he had become the first City player to score at the tournament, a historically rare occurrence for City players (remember Niall Quinn's?).
By the end of the group stage, half of City's contingent were on their way home, half survived to fight another day. The survivors were soon reduced by one however as the patently unfit Sergio Aguero was effectively ruled out of the tournament.

Ex-City rejects players littered the tournament. Demarcus Beasley appeared for the USA, whilst gorgeous Giorgios Samaras, fresh from Eurovision glory, kept his nerve to steer Greece into the knockout stage. There was Nigel De Jong of course, who managed to kick no one in the chest this time around (the day is young, so to speak). Add to that Jerome Boateng, Felipe Caicedo, Kolo and others I may have forgotten (deliberately).

The Toure brothers were hit with a fresh blow after Kolo had shaken off malaria with their news that their younger brother had passed away after a fight with cancer. They bravely stayed on at the tournament. This wasn't good enough for some people, and nor would it have been good enough if they had flown home. The knives were out for a man that had said something unsuitable having just lost his younger brother. Compassion is in short supply in the modern world. The truth will out and accusations and opinions can then be formed, but now is not the time.

But on the whole, this was a tournament full of joy. Such was the joy at participating in this wonderful tournament that players were throwing themselves to the ground at every opportunity, overcome with emotion. The crowd was even more excitable. A camera panning on a fan's painted face was enough to cue mass hysteria and scenes reminiscent of a royal wedding, their team losing 4-0 to Iran now a mere irrelevance, replaced by seven seconds of fame. The true stars were of course the England fans and the reason was simple – they refused point-blank to participate in any Mexican waves.
#R.E.S.P.E.C.T.

As for the officiating, it was poor, poor, poor.

Luis Suarez encountered more hunger issues as he nibbled on Chiellini's shoulder as Uruguay dumped Italy out of the competition, the buck-toothed nutcase clearly under the impression that chiellini is a delicious pasta dish from Bologna. That was not dandruff on the Italian's shoulders, but shaved flakes of Parmigiano-Reggiano. That's nothing short of entrapment.
 As a result of his subsequent four-month ban, Suarez has now been banned for 34 matches since 2010 without having received a red card. His ban from all football activity means he cannot even play Superstar Soccer on his HTC One. Brutal.

In the end the group stages were less about skill winning through than teams profiting from playing in cooler climes than others. Of the eight teams that played in Manaus for their 1st game, seven lost the next game. European giants (and England) fell at the first hurdle, and the world prepared for the excitement of the knockout stage with no outstanding candidate for the ultimate prize.

But first – Friday 27th June. Black Friday. Nothing, no football, not a thing.

The day football died.

World Cup Review: The Knockout Stages

So with England out with such poor performances that Joey Barton came out of international retirement, and with some big fallers at the first hurdle, the tournament moved onto the tense knockout-stage, where it was winner-takes-all, loser-takes-nothing.

There was little disruption of form at first. All eight group winners made it through to the quarter-finals, for the first time ever. Also for the first time ever, no one complained about the sodding ball. You missed a trick there Hodgson.

The goals dried up somewhat, but the final tally was record-equalling. The best half-hour belonged to extra-time in the Belgium v USA game, not only because it won me a bet, but because it was manic as the USA almost came back from the dead. The spate of extra-times played havoc with sleep patterns across the nation. The only thing more inevitable than the widespread work-time yawning was the predictable comparison between the Americans' work ethic and our pampered English "stars".

Brazil entered into a period of mourning, as Neymar was ruled out of the tournament having had his back smacked during the Columbia match. There was outrage from all quarters at the idea that having tried to kick James Rodriguez out of the game via a process of tactical rotational fouling, that the opposition would retaliate in kind. Who knew?

Having stumbled through much of the tournament, the mourning was complete as Germany racked up a record score in an astonishing semi-final against their shambolic hosts. Brazilian people cried and stuff, and then went home upset. Flags may have been burnt, there may have been riots, there will have been booing, and resignations, and red-faced players. The usual stuff, basically. Brazil showed that singing your national anthem really loudly doesn't win you games after all. What's more, pretending that Neymar had passed away before the match wasn't the wisest of moves. He was probably turning in his grave at the subsequent performance.

Rio Ferdinand was on hand in the studio to discuss what Paul Scholes would have done in any given situation. "What Scholesy Would Have Done" was subsequently released as a book, DVD and board game. The punditry on both channels was not bad for once, some pundits even bothering to do some research, the sombre tone of the BBC in stark contrast to the laid-back on-the-beach pally set-up of ITV, Adrian Chiles' and Gordon Strachan's pasty legs living long in the memory, unfortunately.

In the end, Germany were victorious, due to the profligacy of Argentina players and because a lot of their players are really good. The FA immediately announced a ten-year programme to copy Germany's academy and coaching programmes. Expect this to be shelved when Spain win Euro 2016.

Rio Ferdinand turned up to the final in a sailing jacket, obviously keen to make a quick exit across the Atlantic so he could team up with Harry Redknapp at QPR, and the BBC wowed us to a fascinating documentary called Rio in Rio, in which Rio Ferdinand walked around Rio de Janeiro, a fascinating insight into the mind of the footballer as he marvelled at how colourful and atmospheric the city was. This was part of a series that also included Carlisle in Carlisle, where Clark Carlisle walked round Carlisle, Yorke in York, where Dwight Yorke walked round York, and then there was Jordan in Jordan, (Andrew) Lincoln in Lincoln and the grand finale Charlton in Charlton, which used spurious links to show the ghost of Charlton Heston exploring behind the scenes at The Valley. The BBC received 300 complaints.

Vladimir Putin and Sepp Blatter watched the final together, two men made for each other, using the lack of goals as an excuse to compare furnishings in their respective evil lairs. Putin goes for leopard-prints, Blatter uses dollar bills. The list of other VIP guests included David Beckham, Daniel Craig and bizarrely, Olivier Dacourt and one of the Chuckle Brothers. Dappy from N-Dubz sent his apologies.

Alan Hansen bowed out of the punditry game, one less ex-Liverpool player replaced by, damn, an ex-Liverpool player. What were the chances of that?! Danny Murphy created further outrage by competently co-commentating on matches.

Like in the group stage, City players rarely sparkled. Aguero cried, Zabaleta looked moody whilst Demichelis mourned the loss of his ponytail. Fernandinho was scarred for life by the semi-final spanking, by which time Joe Hart (and James Milner) was already at a pool party in Vegas snogging Jack Wilshere. Only Vincent Kompany escaped relatively unscathed.
And so it's over for another four years, until the cosmopolitan, gay-friendly, inclusive climes of Russia embrace the beautiful game in 2018. Still, beats holding it in a desert. Now that would be really stupid.

THE END – thank you for purchasing the book, I hoped you enjoyed it. Please spread the word and do a little good today….and enjoy what should be an exciting season ahead.

I'll leave you with a little quiz…good luck….

And so to the mid-summer of 2014 and the approach of a new season.

After the unmitigated disaster that was the David Moyes era, an era that lasted nowhere near as long as I had hoped, there was always going to be a positive slant on his successor, and that was only exacerbated by the Glazers hiring someone competent. But the love-in that has greeted Louis Van Gaal in his opening month at Old Trafford has been truly sickening. So to celebrate the constant press orgasms, here is a quiz testing your knowledge of United's manager. Can you guess which facts are real?

Louis Van Gaal Quiz

Louis Van Gaal was the inspiration behind the career of Gerard Pique, after he pushed him to the ground and said he would never be a centre back when aged just 12.

Louis Van Gaal invented pie charts (and not Florence Nightingale, as is widely thought)

Louis Van Gaal is known as The Iron Tulip (TIT)

Louis Van Gaal discovered penicillin and also was instrumental in the eradication of smallpox.

Louis Van Gaal makes all players sit at round tables.

These tables had to be shipped in specially from Germany, as they are not used or produced in this country.

Louis Van Gaal has sent a member of staff abroad to do scouting for a friendly, possibly the first time this has happened in the history of association football.

Louis Van Gaal was the inspiration for the birth of rock and roll music.

Louis Van Gaal monitors players' movements on CCTV.

ESPECIALLY Ryan Giggs.

Louis Van Gaal excels in many sports, from squash to croquet to clay pigeon shooting and is also fluent in 17 (seventeen) languages.

Louis Van Gaal is so meticulous he has changed the grass at the Manchester United training ground.

Louis Van Gaal was recently voted the greatest human ever to have existed in a MORI poll, just ahead of Jesus and Jamie Pollock

Louis Van Gaal is so meticulous that he has a meeting with staff at the end of every day.

It took Louis Van Gaal just two days to work out Phil Jones's natural position.

Louis Van Gaal is so meticulous he insists that his English team's players speak English.

In the Netherlands, it is illegal to raise your voice in the presence of Louis Van Gaal.

Louis Van Gaal's biggest outburst at the press while in charge at the Camp Nou was directed towards a Dutch journalist. After insinuating that Van Gaal had broken a dressing room agreement by detailing his reasons for dropping Rivaldo, the Barcelona manager exploded, shouting angrily in hilariously broken Spanish at his compatriot: "You're very bad! Saying I broke my pact with Rivaldo? I never broke my pact. You're very bad. Very very bad. No, no, no, you're very bad. Very bad! ALWAYS negative. NEVER positive. ALWAYS negative."

Louis Van Gaal has more Twitter followers than Justin Bieber.

At Bayern Munich, Louis Van Gaal proved to his squad that he had balls by dropping his pants in front of everyone.

Louis Van Gaal is the greatest manager to have ever walked the earth.

Answers: Of course, the odd questions are true, the even ones are false.
No, hang on, the other way round…no..oh damn, even I'm confused now……

Printed in Great Britain
by Amazon.co.uk, Ltd.,
Marston Gate.